# CALL OF THE VIRGIN

# AT SAN DAMIANO

# CALL OF THE VIRGIN
# AT SAN DAMIANO

*- The Dawn of the New Reign of Jesus -*

By

JOHAN OSEE

J. M. J. San Damiano Center, Inc.
P. O. Box 94
Natick, Massachusetts    01760

Photograph on the front cover depicts the statue of the Miraculous Madonna of the Roses in the Blessed Garden of San Damiano.

The back cover shows the Well of Miraculous Water which is also enclosed in the Blessed Garden.

**Johan  Osee** is the pen name of a Carmelite priest residing in France. He was a convert to the Catholic Faith .

Almost thirty years ago, on October 16, 1964, the Miraculous Madonna of the Roses first appeared to Rosa. At the onset of these Marian apparitions, Rosa's Bishop was occupied at the Second Vatican Council. In his absence, those in authority conducted a very brief interrogation which was the basis for the statement that 'there was nothing spiritual at San Damiano.' The Bishop merely upheld this  decision, and failed to conduct an official investigation into the facts of San Damiano. His successor did the same.

All the principals involved in this great Marian apparition have since left this earth : Mama Rosa, Padre Pio, and the two Bishops.

We await and accept the final judgment of the Church.

Copyright © 1977

*Library of Congress Catalog Card Number 77-78438*
ISBN  0-8158-0354-0

Come, and let us return to the Lord.
For he hath taken us, and he will heal us:
He will strike, and he will cure us.
He will revive us after two days;
On the third day he will raise us up,
And we shall live in his sight.
We shall know, and we shall follow on,
That we may know the Lord.
His going forth is prepared as the morning
    light,
And He will come to us as the early
And the latter rain to the earth.

- Prophecy of Holy Scripture -

The above photo was taken by
Mr. Lucien Boucquey of France
at San Damiano on November 27,
Feastday of the Miraculous Medal

Joseph GRATECOS                 44, Boulevard Henri IV
Photographe                         PARIS 4ème
Expert pres de la Cour  d'Appel
et le Tribunal de Grande
Instance de la Seine

---

## CERTIFICAT D'EXAMEN

Je sousiggné, Joseph GRATECOS, Photographe inscrit sur la Liste des Spécialistes et Techniciens le plus souvent désignès comme Experts près la Cour d'Appel de Paris, demeurant à Paris 4ème - 44, Bd. Henri IV

Certifie avoir examiné une diapositive, dont la prise de vue a été effectuée avec un appareil bon marché. Elle représente le soleil vue de face, des arbres dépouillés et des personnages en premier plan, dont un porte une bannière. Après un examen approfondi et de forts agrandissements de diverses parties, l'Expert peut dire qu'il lui semble que la diapositive n'a subi aucun truquage.

Ce certificat ne constitue pas une expertise, son auteur n'ayant pas été désigné par une décision de Justice, mais peut être considéré comme un témoignage technique et objectif d'Expert.

Fait `a PARIS, le 27 Janvier 1972

(Signed - JOSEPH GRATECOS)

Joseph GRATECOS                          44, Boulevard Henri IV
Photographer                             <u>PARIS 4ème</u>
Expert, by the Court of Appeals
and the High Court of the Seine

_____

### <u>CERTIFICATE OF EXAMINATION</u>

I, the undersigned, Joseph GRATECOS, Photographer, registered on the list of Specialists and Technicians most often designated as Experts by the Court of Appeals of Paris, and residing at PARIS 4eme - 44, Bd. Henri IV

Certify to have examined a negative taken by means of an inexpensive camera. It represents a full view of the sun, bare trees and persons in the foreground, one of which is carrying a banner. After a thorough examination and considerable enlargements of various parts, the Expert can say that it seems to him that the negative has not been submitted to any trickery.

This certificate does not constitute documentary evidence, the author not having been designated by a decision of the Law, but it can be considered as the technical and objective testimony of an Expert.

Written at PARIS, January 1972

(Signed - JOSEPH GRATECOS)

E. LEITZ-FRANCE                    July  20, 1972
PHOTO CINEMA
C. Pomeyrol, Service Technique Photo

Examen de la diapositive communiquée par Msr.
BOUCQUEY

Il s'agit d'une photographie en contre-jour dans laquelle
on remarque un rayonnement lumineux cruciforme au centre
duquel se trouve une silhouette pouvant facilement être
comparée à celle d'une madone classique.

Il est facile de donner une explication technique du
rayonnement lumineux: il s'agit d'un phénomène de
diffraction de la lumiere à travers une ouverture très étroite
qui est ici celle du diaphragme de l'objectif qui se trouve
fermé au maximum pour photographier le contre-jour. En
général, le nombre de branches du rayonnement lumineux
correspond au nombre de pales du diaphragme iris. Ici le
rayonnement à quatre branches correspond bien au
diaphragme à quatre pales de l'appareil KODAK qui a servi
pour la prise de vue.

Nous avons reproduit ce rayonnement par des essais
ultérieurs mais la tache centrale enigmatique ne s'est pas
reproduite.

Il reste donc à donner une explication admissible pour
la tache centrale.  Ce n'est guère possible sur le plan
technique.  Une seule hypothese avait été primitivement
retenue; celle d'une tache de voile sur le film qui aurait pu
être provoquée par une entrée parasite de lumière dans
l'appareil.  Ces taches de voile ont en effet la même couleur
magenta que la tache centrale qui nous préoccupe.

L'appareil a été confié aux services technique de chez
KODAK qui n'ont décele aucun défaut de ce genre, il s'agit
d'ailleurs d'un entiérement fondu sous pression sans
possibilité d'entrée parasite de lumiere. Par conséquent, la
situation et la forme de cette tache centrale ne peut pas être
techniquement expliquée et il faut logiquement en conclure
que l'appareil a enrigistré un phénomène présent dans la
nature.                    (Signed - C. POMEYROL)

E. LEITZ-FRANCE                                    July 20, 1972
PHOTO CINEMA
C. Pomeyrol, <u>Technical Photo Service</u>

<u>Examination of the negative sent by</u>
<u>Msr. Boucquey</u>

This concerns a photograph taken in half-light in which we notice a luminous brightness, cross-shaped, in the center of which is a silhouette easily comparable to that of a classic madonna.

It is easy to give a technical explanation of the luminous brightness: it concerns a phenomenon of the diffraction of light through a very narrow opening which here, is that of the diaphragm of the lens closed to the maximum in order to photograph in half-light. Generally, the number of branches of luminous brightness correspond to the number of paddles of the diaphragm of the iris. Here, the four branches of brightness correspond well to the four paddles of the KODAK camera used to take this snapshot.

We reproduced this brightness in later tests but the central enigmatic spot did not reproduce.

It remains then, to give an acceptable explanation for the central spot. This is scarcely possible technically. A single hypothesis was originally retained: That of a spot of fog on the film which could have been caused by the parasitic entry of light into the camera. As a matter of fact, these spots of fog have the same magenta color as the central spot which preoccupies us.

The camera was entrusted to the KODAK Technical Service who discovered no fault of this kind; moreover this concerns a camera which was entirely formed under pressure, without the possibility of a parasitic entry of light.

As a consequence, the position and form of this central spot cannot be explained technically and it must be logically concluded that the camera recorded a phenomenon present in nature.

(Signed - C. POMEYROL)

## MESSAGE OF SISTER LUCY

- Given in 1961 to Father Agostino Fuertes, Promoter of the Cause of Beatification of Jacinta and Francesco. -

"Father, the Madonna is very displeased, for no consideration has been given to her message of 1917. Neither the good people, nor the wicked pay any attention to it, the good go on their way without concerning themselves and not listening to the heavenly rules; the wicked travel the wide road of perdition, giving no consideration to the punishments which threaten them.

Believe me, Father, the Lord will punish the world very soon. The punishment is imminent; the material punishment will come very soon. Think, Father, of all the souls falling into hell and that will happen because there is no prayer and no penance. All of this is the reason for the Holy Virgin's sadness.

Father, tell everyone that the Madonna told me often that many nations would disappear from the face of the earth. **If we do not obtain the conversion of Russia through prayer and the Sacraments, Russia will be the scourge chosen by God to chastise humanity.**

Tell them, Father, that the devil is undertaking the decisive battle against the Madonna. What afflicts the Immaculate Heart of Mary and the Heart of Jesus is the fall of religious and consecrated souls. The devil knows that in abandoning their beautiful vocation, they drag numerous souls to hell with them. We have at our disposal two very efficacious means of stopping the punishment from Heaven: prayer and sacrifice. The devil does everything he can to distract us and to remove our taste for prayer. We will save ourselves or we will damn ourselves together.

**Father, tell the people that they should not expect a call to penance and prayer from the Sovereign Pontiff, nor from the Bishops, Pastors, or from the General Superiors. It is high time that each one, on his own initiative, accomplishes good and holy works and reforms his life according to the desires of the Madonna.**

The devil wants to seize the souls of the consecrated; he tries to corrupt them in order to harden the others in final impenitence. He uses all the tricks, even going so far as to suggest abandoning the religious life; there results a sterility of the interior life and a coldness toward the laity on the subject of the renouncement of pleasures and total immolation to God. Tell them, Father, that two things contributed to the sanctification of Jacinta and Francesco: The Affliction of the Madonna and the vision of hell . . .

The Madonna finds herself between two swords; on one side, she sees humanity stubborn and indifferent before the announced punishments; on the other, she sees those who profane the Sacraments and scorn the approaching punishments, remaining incredulous, sensual and materialistic.

The Madonna expressly told me: **"We are approaching the last days . . ."** She told me this three times.

**The first time,** she confirmed that the devil has begun the decisive battle . . . Either we are with God or we are with the devil.

**The second time,** she repeated that the final remedies given to the world are the Holy Rosary and devotion to the Immaculate Heart of Mary. Final, means that there will be no other (remedies).

**The third time, she told me that the other means, being disdained and exhausted by men, she is giving us, trembling, the last anchor of salvation, THE HOLY VIRGIN IN PERSON.**

**The Madonna said further that if we do not listen and continue to offend her, we will no longer be pardoned."**

(Extract from the Messenger of the Heart of Mary, August, 1961; published at Rome with official authorization.)

\* \* \*

San Damiano is seen as the fulfillment of the Madonna's words to Lucy: "giving us the last anchor of salvation, **The Holy Virgin in person."** For at San Damiano, the Madonna constantly insists upon her actual presence. A very few of her words in this respect are as follows :

"I AM HERE BEFORE YOU, ALIVE AND REAL, AS IN HEAVEN."
June 3, 1966

"I AM HERE, ALIVE AND REAL, IN YOUR PRESENCE."     June 10, 1966

"I AM IN YOUR MIDST, TRULY ALIVE."
April 19, 1968

Jesus affirms His Mother's presence at San Damiano :

"I HAVE COME TO ACCOMPANY MY HEAVENLY MAMA AND YOURS, TO TELL YOU THAT YOU MUST COME HERE CLOSE TO MY HEAVENLY MAMA WHO WILL GIVE YOU MUCH COUNSEL, MUCH CONSOLATION.    SHE IS HERE IN YOUR MIDST, LIVING AND PRESENT."

The Heavenly Mother :

"Many have forgotten me, they have lost constancy notwithstanding all the graces I have poured upon them with my motherly Heart.    This is why I rely on your fidelity, your help, to make me known and to affirm my presence on earth :
I REPEAT, MY PRESENCE ON EARTH !
I am in your midst and my motherly cry is calling all my children.    I want to save all of you !  Help me !  Help me !  Receive my loving call."
September 3, 1967

# CONTENTS

To Save Souls for Eternity
To Save the Church of Peter
To Postpone the Chastisements
To Prepare Souls for the Triumph of Mary
and the Reign of Jesus

# INTRODUCTION

Something new and great has taken place on this earth: San Damiano. The Virgin Mary has been coming there faithfully and constantly since 1964. She is calling all her children of the entire world to her feet to give proof of her maternal love, to save souls for heaven, to call them to purity, to love, to humility, to charity, to goodness, and to unite them all around her in prayer and sacrifice to save the world.

Appearing from the beginning to a humble peasant, the Virgin would declare that her Son Jesus can no longer carry the Cross, that all must be converted, all must pray and return to God. She would proclaim that she would continue to come always, every Friday, and that after the death of her 'instrument', she would come every First Friday of the month until the end of the world; that her Place is there (San Damiano,) chosen by the Eternal Father in order that she may accomplish her mission as Merciful Mother close to all Her children, to console them, love them, guide them, pardon them and save them.

Ridiculed at first, as often happens, these Apparitions, this Presence of the Virgin Mary, Mother of the Church and of the entire world, can no longer be suppressed. The Virgin Mary summons her children to unite themselves in love around the Holy Father, who is the visible Head of the Church on earth.

Nothing has been able to prevent pilgrims from coming by the tens of thousands from all parts of the world, their numbers growing more numerous year after year. They come, they pray, they accept the difficulties of their journey, they are peaceful, return in thanksgiving and come back again. There is no place on earth where there is so much prayer, day and night. The fruits of conversion, of sanctity in families, in religious vocations, are innumerable. The Madonna is a loving and good Mother.

Objective and clear information concerning these facts is necessary before all consciences. Such is the purpose of this book.

## Prudence

Restrictive measures were taken by the local Bishop, bringing to mind that the same dispositions in various degrees were directed toward previous Marian Apparitions (La Salette, Lourdes, Fatima, etc.) **Competent Vatican authorities have absolutely not intervened. To this day, they have rendered no judgment, no decision on the Apparitions of San Damiano and for the moment seem to have no intention of making any pronouncement.** No one then, would know how to invoke such a pronouncement to condemn pilgrims who go to pray at San Damiano. It is fitting to retain an objective, serene and respectful attitude in this instance, as in all things, concerning the facts and persons involved.

## Means of Access and Accommodations

To arrive at San Damiano from countries outside of Italy, one books air-flight to Milan and from Milan, one can take the train or arrange for private transportation to Piacenza, about a two and one-half hour drive. At Piacenza, there are buses and taxis going to San Damiano which is approximately twelve miles to the south. Driving from Piacenza, one takes the road marked "Val d'Arda." Entering San Giorgio, one turns off and takes a right to Centovera. At Centovera, one takes a right which is a smaller road leading to San Damiano.

The Virgin Mary has promised particular assistance to pilgrims if they pray during their travels.

Although there are two Pilgrim Houses of Saint Joseph and a privately owned hotel, accommodations at San Damiano are somewhat limited, especially on the occasion of Feast-days of the Church. However, there are several hotels in Piacenza offering fine accommodations. During the warm weather, camping facilities are available at the City of Roses. Meals are served in the restaurants at San Damiano.

# CHAPTER I

## THE REALITY OF SAN DAMIANO

**The Place**
"All must know that I come in this place, sent by the Eternal Father, to save you, to enlighten you, to love you!" (April 19, 1968)

San Damiano is a small Italian village situated within the confines of the Emilie and Lombardie Provinces, fifteen kilometers south of Piacenza and seventy kilometers southeast of Milan.

The Apparitions of the Virgin Mary have been taking place in this village since October 16, 1964, Apparitions which one will comprehend to be the most important the world has ever known. The Virgin Mary has already intervened at La Salette, Lourdes, Fatima, to cite but a few of the principal great Marian Apparitions of modern times. "I have been on this earth for such a long time to save my sons!", the Madonna would say. (September 7, 1967)

Today, she comes to San Damiano but in a new manner, in the importance and extent which these Apparitions assume. She strongly insists upon her Presence in this place, sent by the Eternal Father to save all her children, all, the wicked and the good: "The Eternal Father has sent me in this place to convert, to save, to love." (September 8, 1968) "The Madonna says that she does not want to see even one of her sons going to perdition, not one! She wants them all in Paradise with her, for she is the Mama of all, the good and the wicked. She listens attentively to everyone." (August 20, 1965) "I come here to convert souls, to save them, to bring them to Heaven. It is for this purpose that I come." (October 13, 1967)

She calls all her children of the entire world to her feet to unite themselves to her in love, in continual prayer, reparation for offenses, conversion, and to receive in abundance the graces of mercy, comfort, sanctity, Faith, Christian perseverance, and above all, the grace of eternal salvation: "These roses are (signify) all the nations present.

1

I embrace them all, I hold them tightly. I want no one to be lost: neither those present nor those far away. I want them all close to me." (September 8, 1967) "My children, I call many souls into my Presence: many souls that I love, to unite them in prayer and sacrifice to save the world." (September 22, 1967)

Indeed, pilgrims flock to San Damiano from all parts, from all continents and here prayer rises with fervor and in meditation such as in no other place in the world. The silence and prayer at the Place of Apparitions necessitates a respectful attitude at all times; women wear head covering. Conversions are numberless, those of young people in particular, as are also the calls to holy vocations, the fruits of reconciliation in families and peace in hearts:

"It is necessary that people know all that I have done here by my Presence. I have poured out so many, many graces! Such graces! Such conversions! Such material graces! Such spiritual graces!" (September 8, 1967)

This is a holy and blessed place where grace flows in torrents; the place of her Presence, blessed and consecrated by the Eternal Father; the place where the Madonna remains to call souls of the entire world and save them: "This place has been blessed by the Eternal Father." (April 14, 1967) "This is a place of rest, joy and triumph." (December 22, 1967) "Do not abandon my place! It will be the place of refuge, the place of love, tranquility, goodness, sweetness, where I will cover you with my mantle and clasp you in my arms." (April 5, 1968)

**The State of the World**

"The world is in the process of rolling toward the abyss. How many souls are being lost, rushing forward into hell !"
(April 14, 1968)

Truly, the souls of the entire world are in very great trouble in this hour and we must not be astonished that Heaven intervenes and multiplies its calls: "Do you not see how the world is in danger? Do you not see how the world is plodding in mud? In grave sin, especially against purity!" (May 31, 1970)

The world can no longer distinguish between good and

evil, tasting the forbidden fruit without scruple: "There are many souls in tribulations, in afflictions, in error, and they no longer understand either good or evil. There are many being lost in vices and this transpierces my Heart!" (November 29, 1968)

The world has uprooted its principles of truth, Faith and morals, received at a great price during past centuries. In such a climate, neither nations nor persons have a reciprocal confidence and nothing can be enlightened through love. The young people no longer know where truth is to be found in such a milieu. They no longer know if there is truth or hope and have ceased to believe in a genuine love, having never encountered it. Many have never been loved. Everything is offered for their pleasure, liberties and sin; everything is offered to them without guidance or instruction by guides and teachers who themselves are in doubt. They drink from any source and become intoxicated from a poisoned world.

Men are in such deep sin that they no longer see it. Many ask themselves what this word means, they no longer know that sin exists. Immorality, impurity, brutal and cruel selfishness, violence and foolish arrogance are spewed forth without restraint. The Devil has reinstalled himself on earth and reigns everywhere.

**God of Love**
> "Yaweh! Yaweh! Merciful and Compassionate God, light in anger and rich in goodness!"
> (Exodus, ch.34)

The Eternal Father is Father: Father of tenderness and compassion. He does not abandon His creatures who have come from His Creative Power and Love. He sends the Virgin Mary, Mother of all her children here below, all human beings, to draw the souls of the world from sin, she who has received from God the power to crush the head of the serpent and who became the Mother of all at the foot of the Cross where she offered her Only Son for the salvation of all her children.

"The Father, the Son, and the Holy Spirit permit the Mother of all to walk on earth because she wants to save her sons. She loves them so much, with so great a love!" (November 22, 1967)

She comes to bring souls back to the world of God, to bring souls back to the Heart of God, in order to heap the richness of the Love of God upon them, to enliven them with all treasures, joyful in the Heart of God. "Where sin has abounded, grace has super-abounded," says Saint Paul. (Romans, ch.5)

The Virgin Mary comes anew to proclaim Love on earth, as the dawn of the New Reign of Love of Jesus. She comes with more mercy than ever at the threshold of these great hours to love her poor children in their distressing struggle. She comes to save, she comes to pardon, she comes to console: "I am the Mama of Love, of Mercy, of Pardon, of Consolation, of all. A Mama does everything for her children." (October 17, 1967)

She calls: she calls souls to Jesus. If she announces the coming of chastisements on the world as she has in other places in the past, she announces her Triumph even more, the Triumph of her Immaculate Heart, the New Reign of Jesus, the Great Light which will be given in the world. She speaks of Heaven in a manner previously unknown to us:

"When your last hour comes, I will embrace you and clasp you to me. I will take you into the Glory of the Father. You will then see an immense Splendor and numerous souls who will smile and sing your entrance into the heavenly fatherland. When you will see the Splendor of God, you will never have a happier day! What joy you will experience, my sons, when you see my face, when I embrace you to give you the kiss of love for all that you will have done and suffered . . You should triumph with Jesus and sing the Glory of God." (April 14, 1968)

She recalls that the Church of Peter has always triumphed and affirms that it will triumph always. She gives evidence of her motherly love to all her children, the good and the wicked, as she says, wanting all to be saved, for all are her children. She wants purity, humility, goodness and Faith, especially for the young people. She comes to save souls for eternity.

**The Virgin's Words**          "The Eternal Father wants to
punish you. He is weary, He is
weary! Because you pay no
attention to my motherly word!"
(March 8, 1968)

Close to us, the Virgin Mary insists upon her words.
Indeed, she herself is the most pure image of Jesus and her
word is the most pure reflection of the word of Jesus.
Furthermore, for we human beings, the word of our Mother is
dear to us in all things. Let us listen to her:

"I come to bring peace, love, mercy, for all my children."
(November 7, 1969)

"I am here to cover you with my mantle, to clasp you to
me, to fill you with graces and sanctity." (February 11,
1970)

"Extend your arms and open your hearts, here at my
feet: I, who am alive and real as you, welcome you in my arms!
You are all my children whom I love so! I am Mother, I am
Queen and Mother of Love, Mother of Graces. I want all my
children to come under my mantle to protect and save them."
(May 31, 1968)

"I have come to save you, to give you much love, mercy,
because I am the Fountain of Mercy, of Grace, of Pardon, and
the Mother of Consolation. I want to console all those who
moan, all those who weep, who despair." (August 19, 1968)

"My children, I am the Mother and Queen of the entire
world, who comes to console you and to bring peace and love
into your hearts. Open your hearts! Open them with great
Faith! Pour your heart out! Express your desires, all your
cares. Place them all in my Heart and I will do everything
for you." (August 3, 1968)

"I am the Immaculate Conception. I am the Mother of all,
who loves you so much! I come to save you. I come to love
you. I come to console your hearts, to cure your infirmities
of soul and body. I come to sanctify you, to prepare you for
the way of Heaven where Jesus calls you, where Jesus awaits
you one day, above in Paradise." (February 11, 1969)

"I want you to come to my feet to ask pardon, to love me,
to thank me for the many graces I have given you. My
children, put my motherly words into practice, console my
Heart which is so transpierced, for very sad hours are

5

approaching. Unite yourselves in prayer, in love! Hold your Rosary tightly in your hands and repeat it often! It will be your support, your encouragement in the trials. Be united! Be united, my children! It is the reunion in prayer that will save you, that will defend you, that will bring you into the Glory of Paradise beside me.

What joy you will experience in the hour when you depart from this earth if you have done your duty as father, as mother, as son, as consecrated! When I come to take you in my arms to give you the kiss of love, of pardon, what joy you will experience in your heart!

Listen to me! Listen to me, my children! I come on this earth to save you, I repeat. I come in the Name of the Eternal Father. If you ask, you will obtain as Jesus said: Insist, and you will find; knock, and it will be opened to you; ask, and you will receive. But you must ask, you must knock, you must implore." (May 31, 1970)

**The Presence**  "My children, do not fear concerning my Presence. I am among you, alive and real. Do not place any obstacles before these Apparitions which are great, great! I have come at the command of the Eternal Father." (April 19, 1968)

The Virgin Mary comes at San Damiano, alive and real, in the midst of her children. While Rosa was still living, she came not only every Friday at noon but also on each Feast-day of Jesus or Mary, such as the Feasts of the Presentation of Mary in the Temple or of Christ the King, or the Purification of the Virgin, for example. She came as well every day in May, always at the same hour, noon. Finally, she also came on the First Saturday and first Sunday of every month, giving a message each time. Thus, during the month of May, there was a visit and a message from the Madonna each day. Further, it often happened that during the course of the year, the Virgin came several times during the week. And on the many other occasions when the Virgin Mary came, Rosa would announce her Presence when she was still permitted to do so: The Virgin would come during the course of a procession or during a day of prayer and also during nights of prayer preceding great Feast-days and especially, when the pilgrims pray(ed) with great Faith and great generosity.

At one time, the Virgin Mary explicitly announced: "A very great number of foreign pilgrims have prayed all night close to the Enclosure of the pear tree. I was present here. I watched with you, my children, with all the Angels and all the Archangels. I watched with you the whole night. I assisted you and protected you." (March 25, 1968)

It will be noted that the word "appear" is not readily used, but rather the word "come." It must be understood that there is a very great difference between "apparition" and "presence." Persons can have a vision of the Madonna or of Jesus without experiencing the real presence of the one seen. (A rough illustration of this would be watching a person on television; the person is not "truly present" in our room.) These "apparitions" with which certain souls are favored are assuredly supernatural. God permits that they see Jesus or Mary appear to them, smile at them and speak to them, for their good, their instruction or their comfort. Such graces are frequent in the lives of the saints and many other fervent souls. It is a vision, an apparition, but not a presence.

At San Damiano, on the other hand, the Virgin has constantly declared that she was present, and she has repeated this with the greatest insistence: "I am here in your presence;" "I am here, alive and real as you;" "I have come in your midst;" "This is my place;" etc. (From numerous messages.)

Several announcements are even more clear:

"My children, these are days which inflame me with love, seeing you coming here in my Presence, I, who am alive and real as you; I, who see you with my eyes, see your heart, see into your heart and your conscience." (October 27, 1967)

"I have left my Son there, in Heaven, where I reveled in eternal felicity, to come and save you." (December 15, 1967)

"I come from Heaven to return among you." (April 19, 1968)

However, apart from the privileged moments when she descends here below in her little Garden of Paradise, the Virgin Mary remains spiritually present in this place, night and day - a spiritual but an intense Presence, knowing hearts intimately and pouring abundant graces upon her children whom she surrounds with her look of motherly love.

This is her place, her place of grace and love 'par excellence' where she calls her children, where she finds them and presses them to her Heart at every moment, where she acts in souls, where she diffuses her treasures of mercy and tenderness in extraordinary fashion according to the Mission and the Gift that she has received from the Eternal Father for the salvation of all her children here below. It is in this sense that she proclaimed:

"I will be with you in this sacred place day and night, in this little Garden of Paradise." (September 16, 1968)

# CHAPTER 2

## THE HISTORY OF SAN DAMIANO

### Rosa Quattrini's Childhood

The Virgin Mary chose a simple peasant as her instrument, a mother of a family, a woman of sound and simple intelligence, known for her ignorance of worldly things but also for her sincerity, charity, courage and piety. One will come to know her in the following pages through her prayers to the Madonna and Jesus. One will recognize this mixture of simplicity and firmness which characterizes most of the souls habitually chosen by the Virgin Mary as instruments in her interventions upon earth; let us recall Bernadette, the children of La Salette and those of Fatima.

Born January 26, 1909 in the village of Santimento di Rottofreno which is twenty kilometers from San Damiano, Rosa experienced suffering during every phase of her life. Her father died of pneumonia when she was scarcely two years old. Her mother had borne seven children into the world but only four survived; two sons and a daughter died very young. Of these four surviving children, all girls, Rosa was the second-to-last.

Rosa's three sisters all became nuns; Rosa was the only one who married. But this is what God willed for a mission that would consecrate her more highly than any other to Jesus and for the salvation of souls.

The little family left the village of Santimento soon after the death of Rosa's father. They lived on the outskirts of the village of Mirafiore for several years, then changed their residence again.

Rosa's education was quite strict, a strictness which Rosa specified was not due to unkindness but to moral strength. During her youth, Rosa consecrated herself to the catechetical instruction and Christian education of the young within the framework of Catholic works in her parish. With reference to this fact, we wish to point out the following note of interest:

Contrary to what occurred later in life because of continued sickness, Rosa was very quick to learn and retained what she learned. She knew the Mysteries of the

9

Rosary and many prayers. She earned first prize in catechism every year and received a reward of one lira, the same as her sisters. Their mother bought their clothing with these few lire. These examinations and rewards took place around Christmas. Later, repeated sieges of poor health together with all kinds of prolonged treatments and bodily deficiencies diminished Rosa's memory, such as we will see concerning the Mysteries of the Rosary which she could not remember.

From the beginning of the Apparitions, Rosa possessed a normal memory and good intellectual faculties, rapidly discerning the essentials of things and situations.

Rosa was married on Sunday, October 7, 1937 the first Sunday of the month of the Rosary, taking as her spouse Giuseppe Quattrini, a man of lively and simple faith raised, as she, in traditional piety.

She recalled that all the young people whom she had instructed in the catechism and parish works were present in the Church at her marriage and that "they all received Communion, all around me," and that the Pastor had distributed sugar plums after the ceremony.

Rosa had never been to the cinema or theater and saw only one film in her life, after she was married. It had been announced beforehand that the film was about the Apparitions of the Virgin Mary at Lourdes, but in fact the film was changed and a film on war and bombings was shown in its place. The war had greatly affected Rosa and she cried during the film.

Shortly after their marriage, Rosa and Giuseppe came to live at San Damiano. It would be some years later that, obeying the Madonna's counsel, they would move to another house in San Damiano which would be their permanent residence.

It must be mentioned that Rosa loved her husband very much. She was particularly sensitive to the fact that he was the first to believe and accept the Apparitions of the Madonna. There was never any hesitation on his part. This was an immense comfort to Rosa. She called him "Pino," a diminutive of Giuseppino; "He is my Pino," she would say.

God called Giuseppe Quattrini to Him on March 31, 1972; his body rests in the little cemetery of San Damiano.

## The Cross in Rosa's Life

We can speak only discreetly of Rosa's life. All the trials which marked her cannot be revealed. However, it is a duty of truth to make known those trials of decisive importance which could not be hidden without deforming the reality of her vocation.

Rosa always knew poverty, a poverty borne with dignity. Although reticent about these things, she conceded that during her childhood she never received any gifts or toys; such was also the case during her life as mother of a family when great poverty often approached misery.

Suffering has been her lifetime companion, a life constantly filled with all kinds of sorrows. She endured cruel physical suffering and repeated sieges of poor health, occurring at the births of her children. It is necessary to specify the following facts which were discussed with Rosa:

Rosa underwent a painful cesarian operation for the birth of her first child. It was the same with the next two births. These operations were not successful insofar as the closure of the wounds; five wounds remained unhealed. This caused numerous complications: peritonitis, infection, prolonged stubborn high fevers difficult to treat, without counting the multiple series of repercussions on the system of a body so mutilated in its essential organs. These wounds would not close. After the birth of her third and last child, Pier Giorgio, Rosa continued to alternate between home and hospital. During the ensuing years, she spent much time in the hospitals where every treatment was tried on this poor martyred body. She had many blood transfusions and at one time, a complete blood transfusion. In still another clinic, she was given injections which caused much harm, leaving her more dead than alive. Finally, they brought her again to Piacenza where they found her condition to be so desperate that they sent her home to die, as is done in such cases. She was in this condition when the Virgin Mary came and cured her.

We know that Jesus gives the cross to carry in proportion to the mission that souls have to fulfill on earth. Rosa's mission was not only to transmit the words of the Madonna, but also a mission of suffering to save numerous souls and to merit numerous graces linked to the incomparable work of the Virgin Mary at San Damiano and to her Triumph in all hearts.

Rosa was silent concerning her physical and moral sufferings. Like those who possess great purity of heart, she was greatly moved by sad situations and harsh incidents. She wept but only when she was alone, most often at night. Then, before everyone, she resumed her smile and her encouraging and touching words of humility. No one suspected the cross hidden by the smile and affectionate words. She told her intimate friends that many times she offered a night of suffering to obtain grace for a soul.

It must also be said that if the visits of the Blessed Virgin and Jesus are always a great grace and comfort, they were also often a source of great sorrow, at least for Rosa. How indeed could Rosa be happy and joyful when during the preceding night or during noon prayers, she had just seen the Most Blessed Virgin Mary weeping over the sins which offend her Son, transpierce her Heart and cast souls into hell? . . . Or when she had seen the horrible imminent chastisements and the crimes being committed against the innocent? These things left her lifeless and broken. But she said nothing.

**Rosa's Miraculous Cure**

It was September 29, 1961, the Feast of Saint Michael the Archangel. Rosa had been recently returned from the hospital in Piacenza and was in bed on the first floor, suffering greatly. (This house, where the Quattrinis lived prior to moving to their permanent home, is often visited by pilgrims. It is situated about 100 meters from Rosa's present home, beyond the terrain and to the rear of the Enclosure of Apparitions.)

Following is an account of what took place on this particular day in September, taken from the book on San Damiano by Jean-Gabriel. On this occasion, as in succeeding events, Padre Pio's intimate connection with the Apparitions is most evident.

"I was lying in bed and couldn't move. My husband had gone to look for chestnuts.* Only my Aunt Adele was home. It was a hot day. ( * A source of food to augment their meager diet.)

A young woman came around noontime and asked for an

offering. She wanted to light three candles, three little lamps in the Sanctuary of Our Lady of Grace at San Giovanni where Padre Pio was. It would cost 500 lire.

Aunt Adele said, "But we are very poor! Between us, we have 1,000 lire (approximately $1.50 American) at home and even this was borrowed!"

The lady said, "Nevertheless, you should make the offering."

"I've always given offerings," saint Aunt Adele, "but today, we really cannot. My niece, Rosa, is there, suffering the pains of hell; she must be taken care of and we have only these 1,000 lire."

"Where is your niece?", asked the lady.

"She is there," answered Aunt Adele.

Then the lady came in and saw me lying in bed.

"Come, courage! What is the matter with you?", she asked me.

"I am all torn open," I replied. "They brought me home from the hospital because there's no more hope."

At this moment, the noon bell began to ring. Then she said to me, "Come, get up!"

"I can't," I answered.

"Give me your hand," she said.

I gave her my hand but it was useless.

Then she said to me, "Give me both your hands."

I gave her both my hands and I felt a great shock.

"Come, get up!", she told me again.

I got up. I was cured!

I began to shout, "I'm cured! I'm cured!"

But she said to me, "Be quiet!" She then directed me to recite the Angelus and five Paters, five Aves and five Glorias for Padre Pio's intentions.

I recited them and then she placed her hands on my wounds and the wounds healed instantly!

(Rosa was asked about this lady, what she was like. "Her face was very beautiful," said Rosa. "She was dressed as a peasant. She said that she came from very far away.")

The lady then said, "You must go to Padre Pio."

"With what money?" I asked. "The landlord has taken everything."

"You must not stay here," she replied. "Find another house. Then you must go to Padre Pio."

"But I have no money, none for either food or clothing for the trip."

"Do not think about it," she replied. "At the proper moment, you will have all that is necessary."

Indeed, a short time later, I received a letter, with no name, which contained money for the trip.

Two hours before I was to leave, I received two dresses as well. Who knows who sent them? . . . because they fit me perfectly! In the meantime, my Aunt had gone upstairs to get 500 lire and gave them to the lady. Then the lady went away. My little boy, Pier Giorgio, who was playing outside, saw her quite well as she was leaving. There were also other people outside but they did not see her. Only the child saw her. That is how she left.

When I went to San Giovanni Rotondo on a Saturday morning, she reappeared to me there, on the Church plaza.

"Do you recognize me?", she asked. "Make it known now that I am the Mother of Consolation and of the Afflicted. After Holy Mass, I will conduct you to Padre Pio who will give you a mission to accomplish."

> - Extract from Presence de la Très Ste. Vierge
> by Jean Gabriel - Editiones Latines, pp.14, 15,
> with the author's consent.

## Mama Rosa's Life Between
## Her Cure and the First Apparition
## - Padre Pio's Directives -

Guided by the Madonna, Rosa went to Padre Pio. She informed him of these events, notably the Apparition she had just witnessed on the Church plaza.

"Return home, take care of the sick; I will help you." Padre Pio said.

Obedient to this directive, Rosa returned home and began her mission to the sick. She confided to a priest that Padre Pio did indeed help her! As she would set out in faith to accomplish this directive, Padre Pio would come along the road and indicate homes where there were sick people in need of help saying, "Go in this house." "Go here." "Go there." And thus she went to the hospital in Piacenza, to the Charitable Institution. She did not merely visit these places but remained several days. Then she would return home to change her clothing and return again to the spiritual and physical care of the sick. The Rosary was Rosa's constant companion, a means through which much spiritual good was obtained for those she tended.

She lived in this manner for approximately two and a half years. At this time, Aunt Adele became ill with bronchitis. Padre Pio then told Rosa, "Your mission of helping the sick is finished. Return home and take care of your Aunt." He also told her that she was to await "a great event."

We see from this history that Padre Pio was closely associated with San Damiano from the very beginning; and at a later date when problems were encountered in the excavation of the well of Miraculous Water, it was he who offered the solution to the difficulties.

A statue of Padre Pio has been placed close to the Heavenly Mama's 'little Garden of Paradise' to commemorate the very important role he played in the events of San Damiano.

During the time of Rosa's ministry to the sick, she prayed to the Madonna at night. It was then that the Madonna said that one day she would see the field between her house and the road all filled with little houses. These little houses would later prove to be the house trailers of pilgrims. Rosa had never seen one before! Also during this period Rosa learned anew the Mysteries of the Rosary with supernatural assistance. She had been unable to remember them since her long illness. The following account is an extract from the book by S. di Maria:

"One day, as Mama Rosa was completing preparations for dinner, a young priest of about thirty years of age entered and asked if he could pray with her; she assented.

Fascinated by his beautiful prayers, she finally said: "You are blessed to know how to pray so well! I only know how to say the Rosary and I don't even know the Mysteries. Teach me how to pray in a manner that will please the Lord!"

The priest replied, "Continue to pray the Rosary. This prayer is beautiful and powerful. As for the Mysteries, do not concern yourself; I will send someone who will teach them to you. As for the rest, the more simple your prayer, the more it will please God. Repeat often, 'My God, I love you! Jesus, I love you! Jesus, I thank you! Jesus, I ask pardon!'

Pray thus, according to the moments, and as it comes to your mind."

Rosa said, "I feel that you've done me so much good. Where do you come from?" "I am a Nazarene," the priest replied. Rosa asked again, "Probably you come from Loreto?"

Loreto is well-known throughout Italy and is the site of many pilgrimages. No doubt, Rosa associated Nazareth and Loreto as being one and the same.

"Yes, I live in the House of Loreto," answered the priest. Rosa exclaimed, "Oh, come and see me again!" Then she turned, for the cat had jumped on the table to take something . . . when she looked back, the priest had disappeared.

A short time later, as she was beginning the Rosary, she felt her head held between two invisible hands and she heard a voice repeat the fifteen Mysteries of the Rosary seven times. Since that time, she never forgot them.

Some time later, Rosa asked the Madonna who this priest was. The Madonna, smiling, told her that the "priest" she had seen was Jesus of Nazareth who lives in the Tabernacle of the Holy House of Loreto. She also said that it was the Holy Spirit Who had taught her the Mysteries of the Holy Rosary."

( - Extract from the book by S. di Maria: The Most Holy Virgin at San Damiano, pp.24, 25 - Editions du Parvis, Switzerland.)

## The First Apparition

The First Apparition of the Most Blessed Virgin at San Damiano to Rosa Quattrini took place on October 16, 1964 at the pear tree in her garden.

The noon hour was approaching and Rosa was at home alone. She had just completed several household chores and had also prayed the Rosary with a friend who had since returned home. Giuseppe, Rosa's husband, had gone to work and her Aunt Adele had gone to visit Rosa's daughter.

Rosa's account of this first Apparition is reproduced herewith as given in the book 'Presence de la Très Ste. Vierge a San Damiano' to which we have already referred.

"On October 16, 1964 at noontime (says Rosa) I was here; I was reciting the Angelus. I was right at this table and I was praying when I heard a voice outside calling me, "Come forward! Come, I am waiting for you!" I went out and I saw a big white cloud in the sky with many golden and silver stars and many roses of all colors. A globe came out of the cloud, a red globe, which descended to the pear tree.

Then, the Heavenly Mama came out of the globe, clothed in great light. She had a great mantle and a crown of stars and above her head, a great light. She said to me:

"My daughter, I come from very far away. Announce to the world that all must pray because Jesus can no longer carry the Cross. I want all to be saved: the good and the wicked. I am the Mother of Love, the Mother of all; you are all my children. That is why I want all to be saved. That is why I have come: to bring the world to prayer because the chastisements are near. I will return each Friday and I will give you messages and you must make them known to the world."

Then I said to her, "But how will they believe me? I am only a poor, ignorant peasant. I have no authority. They'll throw me in prison!" She replied:

"Do not fear, because now I will leave you a sign. You will see it: this tree will blossom." ( - End of extract.)

On that very day, the entire pear tree blossomed - and this was the month of October! A few minutes after the Apparition, the pear tree was covered with flowers even though it was still laden with fruit and remained so for about three weeks in spite of the heavy autumn rains: a symbol of abundance of graces of salvation and purity which the Most Blessed Virgin Mary would pour out in this place. Close to the pear tree is a plum tree and the part that had been touched by the Madonna in passing was also very beautiful, covered with white blossoms.

This fact was verified, photographed and commented upon in the local press. There was mixed reaction. But the fact remained: the pear tree had blossomed, contrary to all expectations, out of season and immediately after the Madonna's announcement.

From now on, Rosa must recite the Rosary in this place day and night. The Madonna gave messages on Friday in accordance with the promise she had made: to come to this place every Friday (and after Rosa's death, every First Friday until the end of the world.) She also told Rosa that she would have much to suffer, that she would be constantly assisted by Jesus and Mary and that the whole world would come to this place.

## The First Foreign Visitors

It must be noted that the first foreign visitors to arrive at San Damiano were from Portugal, three cousins of Sister Lucie of Fatima.

## The Unfolding of the First Apparitions

At San Damiano, the Virgin Mary most often designated herself by the sweet name of Heavenly Mama, which name we will retain. Holding to the promise she had made, she appeared the following Friday and since this time, has come and continues to come in her chosen place, place of predilection which she would soon call her 'Little Garden of Paradise," i.e,, garden of innocence, of joy, and of the Presence of God.

For this first official visit, the Heavenly Mama had previously directed Rosa to summon a parish priest from a neighboring village and an officer from the NATO Airbase which was very close to the Quattrini home. The military officer was an American General who came with a good number of servicemen. It is he who, according to the Madonna's Will, recited the first public Rosary at the pear tree during an Apparition. The servicemen knelt at his command; they also were the first pilgrims.

Pilgrims came from San Damiano and surrounding villages in the following weeks. Soon, others were coming from the larger cities: Parma, Pisa, Modena, Bologna, Genes, Pavia. There were especially many priests.

Rosa specified that during this period, the Madonna would often interrupt her message, the message thus assuming the form of a dialogue, as will be seen further on. This message form continued during the following years; there was more spontaneity and Rosa would express herself with great simplicity when speaking to the Madonna or when describing an Apparition. (One of these earlier messages is found further on in this book to illustrate the transition of message form during the later years.) The Heavenly Mama's visit thus easily assumed a conversational aspect.

The Madonna gave many prophetic signs during this

time. She would announce something and it would come to pass as foretold. The purpose of these signs was to help souls in the faith of her Presence in this place. The Madonna also gave many signs in the sky.

Rosa said that during these early years, the Madonna would often walk alongside her when she went to morning Mass and that wherever the Madonna's foot touched the ground, flowers would spring up. Thus, there would be a path of flowers from Rosa's house all the way to the Church door.

During this period as well, the Blessed Virgin told Rosa that the Italian people would not come to these Apparitions but that the whole world would come, from all the nations of the world. Rosa as yet had not received the pilgrims who one day would come in great numbers; she spent her nights at the pear tree praying the Rosary. She was often joined in prayer by the pilgrims, especially priests. Rosa told us that many priests were thus brought back to a more fervent life. A single recitation of the Rosary in this blessed place was a source of privileged graces as is still the case today.

An infinite number of scenes unfolded during these Apparitions which Rosa would relate at that particular time. Many books would be needed to describe all that has taken place at San Damiano through the intervention of Heaven.

Crowds from San Damiano and the surrounding villages continued to come for several weeks, terminating with the first intervention of the Bishop of Piacenza. Then, while the village of San Damiano suddenly seemed to ignore these Apparitions, pilgrims began to come from further away.

There was as yet, no fence around the 'little Garden of Paradise,' there was no 'well of Miraculous Water' and there was no statue of the Miraculous Madonna of the Roses. Rosa and the pilgrims knelt close to the pear tree on the bare ground.

## The Flowering of the Apparitions

The years between 1965 and 1970 can rightly be called a period of flowering, a time when the Apparitions began to be known worldwide. The Apparitions continued at the site with organized prayer - an order necessary for the recitation of prayers and for the freedom of expression of those present at the feet of the Heavenly Mama, whether it be in Rosa's oratory during the day or around the pear tree at the time of the Apparition.

Following the instructions of Saint Michael, all public prayer at the Shrine was to be conducted in Latin to insure a prayerful vocal harmony among the many present who spoke a foreign tongue.

Arriving around the little blessed Garden, the pilgrims would at once feel encompassed by the Virgin Mary's motherly love. Days and nights spent in prayer with hearts irresistibly drawn by the Madonna's sweetness and purity, each one having so many graces to request, so many sorrows to confide to her Heart!

It can be said that in this place, each one feels the pulsations of love of the Heart of the Madonna in one's innermost being. In silence or in the murmur of prayers, hearts are gently set on fire with a love that does not become extinguished.

Public prayer would begin in mid-morning. Beautiful Italian hymns, litanies, invocations, great Christian prayers like the Credo, Veni Creator, Salve Regina, the Pater and Ave Maria were successively prayed or sung with fervor. Then the regular prayers began, recited with order by all: Litanies of the Blessed Virgin, the Angelus, the Way of the Cross. Rosa, consecrating her time and strength during the day to the receiving of pilgrims, would arrive for the Rosary. She would then recite the Rosary in her clear strong voice, filled with tenderness for the Madonna and everyone would respond.

A moment would then come when her voice would become more gentle, more affectionate, in the same way that we would speak to a person whose presence touches our hearts. And this was surely the case: the Madonna was there! Unforgettable moment, moment of solemn and profound welcome and then suddenly, Rosa would be silent because the Virgin was present and was about to speak. Hands bustled feverishly with tape recorders. All hearts were suspended, as it were, to the Heart of the Virgin in an expectation aroused by intense love.

Gently, Rosa pronounced these words that all can recall, "The Heavenly Mama is present . . .," in Italian: "Qua` c'e` presente la Mamma Celeste." Each clearly enunciated syllable, retained in ears and hearts, announced the grace that Heaven was giving in this privileged place in that moment: the Presence of the Most Blessed Virgin Mary.

Everyone present knew he was about to hear the Madonna's own words through Rosa, her dearest daughter and chosen instrument, that they would receive the graces requested and even more - because the Madonna gives much more than we ask for, especially in this Garden of Paradise where the Eternal Father sends her with hands filled with immense graces for her children here below, who are so tormented.

The intimate joy of this meeting, this 'Presence!' A dew of benevolence, an illumination of hearts, a rain of roses, an embrace filled with maternal tenderness. No words can express what the Madonna's visits mean to her children.

The messages were thus made known and generally recorded by some of the people. Aside from the years 1966-1967, all the messages were recorded and consigned.

We take the liberty to state here that it is absolutely impossible to humanly explain the accomplished fact of the messages of San Damiano without the intervention of Heaven. Those who deny the supernatural character of the Apparitions of San Damiano have never been able to give a satisfactory explanation. They have resorted to ridiculous suppositions which they have had to renounce.

All can verify that Rosa has never read a single line of the message as her eyes were always raised toward the Madonna with a beautiful, innocent, tranquil, radiant look; everyone remembers this image.

Memorizing a message each time, i.e., a message prepared by another person for Rosa to make use of, is inconceivable. Were this the case, the person writing the messages would have to possess, at one and the same time, the great purity of heart reflected by these messages and the diabolical scheme of playing a game of supernatural trickery!

We can also reflect upon the following facts: that sometimes Rosa was extremely weary; that she had received pilgrims during the entire day, giving the Madonna's answers to each pilgrim; that she must watch that everything that takes place is in good order; that she has already been present for a whole hour in the midst of everyone reciting the

Rosary in the scorching heat of summer or in the cold of winter; and finally, that the messages are theologically irreproachable, filled with love and wisdom, which cannot come from the devil.

## San Damiano Since 1968 - 1970

The divine action of grace has given a new countenance to this place: more universal, richer in faith and generosity. This is the reality of San Damiano - the Presence of the Virgin Mary in this place, sent by the Eternal Father to save her children here below and to love them with all her motherly love. This reality does not change, would not change and will never change. The Virgin Mary has announced and promised that she would come always in this place, even after Rosa Quattrini's death: "I will come always. The Eternal Father promised this to me: every Friday while my 'instrument' is still alive. Then, I will come every First Friday until the end of the world." (February 19, 1966) She has proclaimed that nothing can oppose her power and that nothing will prevent her from fulfilling her mission as Mother close to her children.

However, circumstances on earth do change and at the beginning of February, 1968 and without anyone expecting it, the Bishop of Piacenza notified Rosa of an interdiction forbidding her to go to the pear tree during the Apparitions of the Madonna. It was an immense sacrifice for Rosa but she obeyed. It was also an immense sacrifice for the pilgrims. Nevertheless, the messages continued to be transmitted.

Secluded within the oratory of her home, Rosa received the messages at the very moment of the Apparition, diffusing them at the same instant to the pilgrims over a loudspeaker. The pilgrims continued to come. Their faith was not shaken, neither their fidelity; they had received too much from the Madonna to abandon her. They continued their pilgrimages in serenity without rebellion or bitterness. The fruits of grace continued to grow in souls.

The following message of December 8, 1968 is important because it contains Rosa's conversation with Jesus and the Heavenly Mama concerning the interdiction of the local Bishop prohibiting her from kneeling at the pear tree at the time of the Madonna's apparition.

Also in this message, the Heavenly Mama speaks of a great Cross that we will see in the heavens :

"I am here among you with my Son Jesus, with all the Archangels, Angels, Thrones and Dominations, with all the Saints, and, above you, the Eternal Father and the Holy Spirit. Jesus is with you, the Heavenly Mama is in your midst, who loves you, smiles at you and gives you so much love and every happiness.

My sons, you who have listened to my motherly invitation, I inundate you with graces today. I give you many graces, very many conversions, much love and the supreme grace to arrive in Heaven. That is what I want, my children.

Be ready, with a sincere soul, with Jesus in your heart. Jesus is the Source, Jesus is the Force, Jesus is Love, Jesus is He Who purifies and sanctifies you for Heaven.

I cover all with my mantle, my children. I pour upon you all the graces that the Eternal Father has given me to come here among you to console my children here below, to fortify them in Faith and Christian love.

Be strong, my children, be strong, for the struggles are approaching, especially for Italy which was my "prediletta." Yesterday, I went through the entire world and the gravest mire, I found in beautiful Italy : so many sins of impurity, so many scandals . . . I cried so . . . Italy was love, Italy was strength, courage, Faith! The Church of Peter is there which must triumph in the world in Christian love . . .

The Faith of Peter, the Church of Peter will triumph! Regardless of what is done, the Church will triumph! She has always triumphed. Jesus is always the Conqueror and He will conquer always. Remember that!

My sons, alone, without my power and the Hand of God, you can do nothing!

Listen to me while there is still time! Prepare yourselves and keep yourselves ready! I have asked the Eternal Father for so much mercy . . . much . . . much . . . much! He will diminish the effects of His Justice a little, but He says:

"Enough! Enough! Enough! For they have not listened to My Word . . . They want to act alone, but alone, . . . No!"

Power is of God. The Greatness . . . of God. The Mercy . . of God. Pardon, it is God Who gives it. Reflect, reflect, my sons, for the hour has struck! Wake up!

My sons of predilection, (priests), whom I love so, wake up, bring love, save the souls that Jesus has confided to you . . . save them . . . save them . . . for there are so many dangers. Approach the young people, go into families and bring the Rosary because it is the most powerful weapon!

(A conversation follows between Jesus, the Most Holy Virgin and Mama Rosa. We mention here only the following passage - Rosa Quattrini asks:)

"Heavenly Mama, I have to ask you something in front of everyone . . . it grieves and saddens me very much because the "Observer" has said that I am not obeying the Archbishop. What must I do? Answer me, Heavenly Mama! Jesus, answer me. I am ready to do only Your Will."

**Jesus:** "You obey the Bishop also because you do not come here on Fridays. (At the pear tree.)  But when I call you, I and My Mama, you must return. You must give love to souls, you must give Faith to souls . . . Do you not see, my daughter, that many 'instruments' of My Mama and yours have become lost, that many are in sin, because they have not obeyed My Mama and yours?"

**Heavenly Mama:** "Now is the moment to recall souls. It is the moment to awaken them, my daughter, to give light to all, love to all. You are here to suffer, to love and to make others love. You will have your greatest joy in Heaven, my daughter. You must not fear. Be strong, strong . . . and do not doubt me and my Son Jesus. Jesus has you in His Side: you are His little creature. I have you in my arms, my daughter."

Rosa: "Yes, Heavenly Mama, I do not doubt; I am ready to accept all that you desire, even death."

**Heavenly Mama:** "My Heart will triumph in the whole world, my daughter. My Heart is great; my Heart is love, my daughter, and Jesus will reign in everything. He will come to reign in the world with all the Apostles who are present here.

Heaven and earth will break loose but afterwards will come the calm. After the storm will come the Light, this great Cross, my children, that you will see in the heavens: This Great Light which will awaken you . . . For those who will have believed, what joy they will have, what love they will have in their heart!

You must not doubt! Advance always, advance always with Jesus and with your Heavenly Mama who loves you so.

Jesus is with you, the Mama is at your side.

Always be serene, my children, always with Jesus, always, on earth, and then you will revel above to sing with the Angels and Saints.

Yes, I have given many graces of conversion . . . the salvation of souls . . . love of souls . . . I have awakened hardened hearts.

Always be united to me, my children, always be united to me and my Son Jesus. Pardon, and you will be pardoned. Love one another, love one another, love one another, my sons! Let there be no discord, no malice, no pride, but only love, as Jesus wants you to be and according to the call of your Mama.

I am the Immaculate Conception. I want you to be as white as snow, as pure as the lily because there is much happiness in a Mama's Heart in seeing all  her sons around her.

I let my Son Jesus die to save you and now . . . to see so many of my children surround me with such great love, such lively Faith . . . Always listen to my invitation! Love one another very much and love my Son Jesus very much."

### Rosa is Silenced

On Thursday, June 4, 1970, the Bishop of Piacenza summoned Rosa to his residence to give formal notice of his interdiction forbidding her to transmit the Madonna's messages, either publicly or privately.

The following day, Rosa informed the pilgrims in these terms at the moment of the Apparition:

"I am informing you that the Bishop has ordered me to no longer transmit the messages of the Heavenly Mama, either publicly or privately. I will obey. I will no longer transmit them. But I do not deny, and will never deny, the Heavenly Mama. I say and will always say that the Heavenly Mama has come, comes, and will always come. Offer, suffer and be silent for the Triumph of the Heavenly Mama. Pardon everyone. In silence, all will be obtained."

The purity of this declaration recalls the attitude of John of the Cross; it was a declaration of the most perfect obedience. By her conformance in this circumstance, as in all things, according to the Madonna's directives, Rosa gave to all an example of irreproachable respect and submission to

Church authority. From that day, the messages were no longer transmitted.

Let us take note of the renewed affirmation of the Presence of the Virgin Mary in this place: "I say, and will always say, that the Heavenly Mama has come, comes, and will always come." It is very clear.

Let us also note the insistence on silence, pardon, the acceptance of sacrifice. Whoever does not understand these things could not have understood the behavior of Jesus on the Cross; they will have understood nothing at all of San Damiano.

Someone else at San Damiano had also been silenced: Rosa's Pastor: Father Pellacani. Because he refused to deny the Madonna's Apparitions to Rosa, he was removed from his parish in 1969 and forbidden to publicly exercise his ministry. Left with no means of support, Father Pellacani returned to the mountain home of his parents, since deceased. This banishment lasted for about fifteen years during which time he offered daily Mass in the privacy of his home. A few years before his death in August, 1989, he was re-instated and given a parish.

After Father Pellacani's removal from his pastorate, he was replaced by Father Segundo. Father Segundo was also later removed because he disagreed when the Bishop ordered the church closed on Pentecost Sunday of a particular year. Finally, Father diCrema commuted daily from Piacenza to say Mass at San Damiano. He has since been appointed Pastor.

Since the beginning of the Apparitions in 1964, there have been three Bishops; two are now deceased. Bishop Mazza is the third and present Bishop of the diocese in which San Damiano is located.

## Father Pellacani's Testimony

"I have had many, many pilgrims in San Damiano say to me, "Here at San Damiano, we have found our spiritual life, our conversion, prayer, sacraments, the Mass; therefore, conclusion, the messages of Mama Rosa have brought many, many people to pray and to take the road of salvation . . .

In my opinion, Mama Rosa is just a poor instrument. In 1961, Mama Rosa had a vision. One morning after attending Mass, she came into the sacristy, "Oh, Padre! Last night I saw the Church filled with many, many people, even to the choir loft! Many, many people outside the Church, and you were hearing confessions and giving many Communions. You were very tired." I said, "Mama Rosa, you are a good woman; you think of the Church, you pray. Your mind is on the Church and you may also pray during the night. Rosa, you had a wonderful dream . . . it is normal to dream. The extraordinary thing is that you thought to come to me to speak of your dream."

She answered, "That is not true! The Blessed Virgin showed me the Church filled with people and she told me to come to you. That is why I came. She said that there would come a day when the Church will be filled with people." "Now, Mama Rosa, you said last night you saw a Church filled with people. Well, now this morning you attended Mass. How many attended Mass?" "Four people, Padre," she answered. And, "How many Communions? Two Communions. Now I say to you: it isn't true you saw the Blessed Virgin . . . a dream is a dream . . . pray very much so that all the parishioners of San Damiano come to Mass on Sunday. That's enough for me! That's my dream!" And she went home.

After fifteen or twenty days, she returned with the same story. I said, "Mama Rosa, you repeat the same dreams, but the odd thing is that you believe your dreams to be real. I cannot understand you." She answered, "But it is the Blessed Virgin who showed me the Church filled with people and she told me to come and tell you that the day would come when the Church would be filled with people"

So, the years went by, 1961, '62, '63, '64, 65. One day, a most amazing thing happened! The Church was filled with people, both inside and outside, not only once but several times! My thoughts went immediately to what Mama Rosa had told me years before.

## Padre Pio Confirms San Damiano

Around the beginning of March, 1965 I brought Mama Rosa to Padre Pio for confession. I also was a penitent of Padre Pio. (Note: Father Pellacani was the head of all Padre Pio activities in that area.) Padre Pio had the stigmata and I do not say this from hearsay. I have seen the stigma and the blood ran from it continuously. When Padre Pio saw a person, he knew all about the person. He performed many miracles, brought about many conversions during his life.

When the Apparitions began, I said to myself, "If there is one on earth who can tell us the truth about San Damiano, it is Padre Pio. I must take Rosa to him." Rosa was willing. At San Giovanni Rotondo, we went on to the confessional. When Rosa was near the confessional, I was afraid, as Padre Pio was an extraordinary confessor who could be very harsh and many times would withhold absolution. He would not hesitate to tell Rosa or anyone if he didn't want you there: "I did not tell you to stand here! Get out, leave!" I tell you, I was afraid. I placed myself at a distance from Rosa. If Padre Pio reprimands her, it is better that I am far away. Although he was saintly, he would reprimand anyone. Finally, Rosa entered the confessional and I felt relieved.

When Rosa came out of the confessional and finished her prayers, I questioned her on what Padre Pio said and if she had mentioned the Blessed Virgin at San Damiano. Rosa replied, "Yes, I did. He said to me, "When you see the Blessed Virgin, pray very much and speak to her of me. I have need of graces. Rosa, you must work, pray, and make sacrifices for the Triumph of the Blessed Virgin at San Damiano." These words of Padre Pio were positive. Padre Pio believed and approved!

Later on, some French-speaking priests came to San Damiano. They told me that they had come here because of the Apparitions of the Blessed Virgin. Before arriving here, they had gone to confession to Padre Pio and asked about the Apparitions of San Damiano. Padre Pio said to them, "You do well; so pray for the Triumph of the Blessed Virgin at San Damiano."

In San Damiano, there have been many extraordinary signs, many unusual photos; many pilgrims have heard the angels singing.

I have been removed from my parish. I have nothing. I do not want to rebel against my Bishop. I simply want to help him find the truth regarding San Damiano. Understand: being a witness for five years, I state that there is the supernatural in San Damiano and I will not deny it. I will not deny the Blessed Virgin and to speak of it to defend the truth is the most important duty in my life! If I had accepted the judgment of my Bishop, I would still have my parish in

San Damiano. In good conscience, it was not possible to deny the truth."

## Rosa's Obedience

Rosa's brief declaration touched only lightly the profound reality of San Damiano:   an abyss of Faith, Obedience and Love, Christian Hope, the source of which can only be the Heart of the Virgin Mary, a delicacy that is not of this world, in the respect of the Church.  For we must reflect upon what was being sacrificed: the word of the Heavenly Mama to her children of the entire world to save them for eternity.  And most certainly, we must remember a fact of quasi-infinite significance, the words of the Madonna: "Reflect!  Reflect!  While there is still time!" (From various messages.)   However cruel the results of this act of obedience, the Madonna who comes to save the Church of Peter and not to destroy it by disputing, asked this sacrifice of her children.

The pilgrims also conformed with the Madonna's request. There was no complaining.  Prayer succeeded prayer.  Love succeeded love.  Grace succeeded grace.

As in all trials accepted with faith, these brought abundant fruits into souls and in things.  Their love became more generous.  Henceforth, they were no longer impelled by any desire for consolation or of curiosity.  Their Faith and their love must be pure and strong and with the grace of God, and so it was.  Union with the Madonna became more intimate, more internal, more spiritual, as did union with Jesus to Whom the Virgin leads us.  We reflect upon the words of Jesus: "When I will have been raised from the earth, I will draw all to Me."

Today, the whole world flocks to the feet of the Madonna at San Damiano from all continents, people of all races.  The Heavenly Mama's first prophetic announcement has been fulfilled.  The Madonna had announced this in the earlier years:  "All will come here at my feet to ask for graces, comfort, consolation.  It is the confirmation, my children, of what I said the first time I came to her who is my 'instrument': All those who are far away will come but those who live nearby will be less numerous because they do not listen to my invitation as Mother, who suffers so for her sons.

But I will pour many graces on the whole world, especially upon those who come from far away, from distant, foreign lands. I will assist them during their travels. I will give them graces, great graces, as well as much power and help to diffuse my motherly word."

In the will to obey the repeated requests of the Virgin, efforts proceeded in the midst of a thousand difficulties for the realization of the works of charity so often requested in her messages. The result has been the acquisition of vast acreage where works continue to progress for the edification of this new Garden of Graces willed by Heaven and which the Virgin has designated under the name **"City of Roses."** It is indeed the City of Love of the Hearts of Jesus and Mary, the City of the Reign of Love of the Heart of Jesus in all hearts where, under the Sun of grace of the Most Holy Trinity, will bloom the flowers of love, purity, humility and charity that Jesus comes to raise up here below in His New Reign.

# CHAPTER 3

## THE MESSAGES

The Most Blessed Virgin Mary has expressed herself at San Damiano and before anything else it is fitting that everyone know her words as she has pronounced them in this place.

As more than one hundred messages were given annually, it is impossible to present all of them in this book. Therefore, messages from different years have been selected which express the constant thought of the Heavenly Mama, her most cherished instructions, her most consistent sentiments.

It is appropriate that several messages given by Jesus be included. Messages were often given by Jesus during the course of the year. Jesus is present on the First Friday of each month and on most of the great Feasts in His honor. Although it would have been more appropriate to first present the messages of Jesus, we have not done so because San Damiano is primarily an intervention of the Blessed Virgin.

As Saint Michael the Archangel has also intervened several times at San Damiano, we are including one of his messages.

During the beautiful period when the Bishop of Piacenza had not yet imposed interdictions, the messages from Heaven were always given in public at San Damiano. Herein is a fact of great importance, before the world and before history: everyone could witness the event, everyone could record the messages. These recordings were never objected to by Rosa and are a completely objective documentary considering the fact that no deviation was ever detected in any of the taped messages. It is evident that these documents were scrupulously examined in the process of transcribing and translating, the greatest care being taken of keeping to the text as literally as possible.

It must be stated that Rosa never read the messages. She was present at the pear tree deep in ardent prayer for more than one hour before the Apparition. Never has anyone had even the slightest impression that she was reciting something that had been memorized. The many private recordings made on a thousand different occasions are there as evidence. Incidentally, one cannot fail to notice the difference between Rosa's ordinary simple language and the style of the messages which, while remaining simple, involve a construction and harmony never utilized by Rosa in other circumstances.

The spirit of the messages of San Damiano is filled with love; it is encouraging, positive, a bearer of confidence and hope, particularly with regard to sinners, even those who most offend Jesus and the Madonna. One will read in the messages: "There are many souls here who have no faith, who curse and mock me. But I hold them in my arms as well. I do not want them to be lost. I want to clasp them very, very tightly. I want them to approach me in faith, in great hope, in ardent charity, for I love you so!" (August 15, 1965)

When the Virgin Mary speaks of sin and sinners, she places greater insistence upon hope and mercy than on judgment and chastisement. It is her motherly duty to warn her children and this she does, but she does so as a Mother. She consoles more than she threatens; she pardons, saves, presses all her children to her Heart and wants to embrace the wicked as well as the good. She wants them all with her in Paradise. These comforting words hold a completely remarkable place in the messages of San Damiano without ignoring or neglecting to mention through silence the salutary fear of the Divine Sentence and the consequences of sin or the fearsome reality of the announced chastisements. Although at times upsetting, San Damiano is the constant language of motherly love; it is realistic, but intensely loving and merciful.

Future events are not presented here in a long and somber description of the Apocalypse. The Triumph of Mary, the Reign of Jesus, the Light which will be given in the world and in consciences, Heaven and the incomparable joy which will be forever, the triumph of the Church and confidence in the Supreme Pontiff hold more of a place in the messages than dreadful descriptions. In this Garden of Paradise, Heaven announces Love, the Triumph, Light and Eternal Joy, not only for a few of the privileged, but in an intense will of Mercy, it is extended to all, whoever they may be.

The doctrine of the messages is the constant doctrine of the Church. There is certainly no other place where the

Credo is recited as much as here. Every teaching of the Faith is recalled in the messages in one manner or another which concern the great Christian mysteries of the Holy Trinity, the Incarnation and Redemption; the teachings of the Gospel - from the childhood of Jesus up to His Ascension; the Sacraments among which the Eucharist holds the highest place as is most fitting; and again, the concern with Christian morals, especially the duties of charity and family morals.

The attitude towards the Church has been one of constant obedience. In this regard, there has never been a negative mood nor has the atmosphere ever been one of painful criticism, as in many other places. The Virgin Mary says and repeats that the Church, the Church of Peter, has always triumphed and will triumph always, in everything and against everything, and the Madonna has always guided her 'instrument' on the way of respect and obedience towards Church authorities. This climate contrasts with the somber language of false messages which abound today. San Damiano appears as a dawn of hope and renewal while remaining fully realistic.

There is no question of a strange, mysterious, particular way in which one must find a salvation reserved, so to speak, for a few of the initiated. The ways are the same as always. They are those of the Church, those of the most steadfast Christian Faith and even what is most imprinted in all hearts: before anything, the state of grace and hope of Heaven: "A good Confession and a good Communion." How many times we have heard these words! The Eucharist and the Rosary, fraternal charity, humility, goodness, an ardent love for Jesus with the remembrance of His life, death and resurrection, much prayer to the Holy Spirit, to the Holy Trinity, Faith, the happiness and joy that comes with the estrangement of sin, recourse to the Angels - these are the Madonna's most steadfast instructions. The Virgin Mary does not come to abolish, but to fulfill and confirm the foundations laid by Christ.

We will examine in one of the following chapters exactly what the messages of San Damiano convey and the great call they proclaim to all humanity.

## Message of the Most Blessed Virgin
### August 15, 1966
#### - Feast of the Assumption of the Virgin Mary -

This message, given on a great Feast-day, is quite lengthy and is marked from beginning to end by a continuous effusion of joy in love. The Heavenly Mama's constant mercy for sinners will be noted, "the wicked as well as the good," the love which is lavished upon them as well as on the others. This is a sign of messages from Heaven.

At the same time, the Madonna recalls the great truths: Heaven, the Sacraments, the theological virtues of faith, hope and charity, the value of spiritual graces, sanctity, eternal salvation, the Angels, etc. The messages of the Madonna are simultaneously an outpouring of tenderness and a catechesis: "full of grace and truth."

"My children, I have come earlier today: it is my Feast-day; . . . with a great company of Angels, Saints, Patriarchs, all the Archangels: they are all present here.

I have come to bring you many graces and blessings and I send you a lovely coolness because you are very, very hot!" (The Blessed Virgin sends a cooling breeze.) "That is why I came. My mantle flutters above you, causing a breeze.

I send you a great rain of graces and blessings. I am here close to you; I watch over you and hold you tightly in my arms. I pass around you, above you. I watch over you, I guide you, assist you, my children. I want so much good for you, so much! I have assisted you all during your journey. I have made your trip one of joy and graces. When you return, I will send the Guardian Angels who will follow you the length of your travels.

Pray, pray with faith! But ask for spiritual graces! As for material graces, I think of them, my children. But very, very few ask me for spiritual graces . . . very few. Everyone asks for material graces.

Do you not know that you are on this earth but for a short time? You must think of eternity, there where I await you, my children. Recite the Rosary, approach the Sacraments, prepare your soul, clearly, sincerely, for your Mama does not abandon you even for a moment. I follow you step by step.

I am the Queen of Heaven, the Queen of the Universe,

Queen of the entire world. I am your Mama who loves you so, the good and the wicked as well. The good are already close to me and I want to clasp the wicked tightly to me.

There are many souls here who have no faith, who curse and mock me. But I hold them in my arms as well; I do not want them to be lost. I want to clasp them very, very tightly. I want them to approach me in faith, in great hope, in ardent charity, for I love you so!

Pray, my children! Pray! Do not doubt me, I am here in your presence. Even though you do not see me, my children, I am here nevertheless. I see you, I follow you. I do not abandon you.

These are graces which you obtained to come here because you would never have been capable of it by yourselves; it is I who accompanied you, who assisted you. Why do you not pay attention to my Presence? Why do you not remember your Heavenly Mama?

Prepare your soul. Prepare it for Jesus by receiving Jesus in the Holy Eucharist, for Jesus does not abandon you. I will inspire you, I will assist you, guide you.

Courage, my children! Courage! This is a world of tears. Everything passes; you must think of eternity, there where I await you. There, you will revel in eternal happiness, if you are prepared . . . Will it be hell or will it be Paradise?

My children, I am the Mama of Love, the Mama of Mercy, the Co-Redemptrix of all. I love you so! **Call me by the sweet name of Mother.** Call me: I am ready to receive your cries, your words. Call me, my children! Call me! Do not wait until it is too late! Call me! I listen to you because I am the Mama of all, who loves you so!

Pray! Pray for all those who are present, for all those far away, for everyone. That all may reconcile themselves with Jesus; above all, those who are dying in this hour and do not want to be reconciled. Call your Guardian Angel so that he goes everywhere, especially to the bedside of the sick who are dying in this moment. Listen to my words: I want them all in Paradise, all.

Today, I am letting fall a great rain of graces from Heaven, a great rain of roses, on all those who are here, on those who are far away, on those who are united in this hour.

My children, ask with faith during the length of your journey, and you will all receive a grace in the Name of the

Eternal Father. Ask for it. Ask for it with faith. I will come close to you, inspire you and I will fill your heart with great peace, much love, much confidence in me.

Be serene, my children. Do not preoccupy yourselves so with material things because everything passes. Prepare yourselves for Heaven: There, you will revel in such happiness! ... in such happiness, my children! You will be there for eternity!

Pray, my children, and ask this grace of Jesus, to arrive in Heaven. Ask with faith. I think of the material graces, my children: do not preoccupy yourselves so. Ask first of all for spiritual graces, the grace to arrive in Heaven; for you are on this earth for such a short time! You must think of Heaven where I await you. Your Guardian Angel will come to take you in his arms and carry you away into the Heavenly Fatherland.

Ask for graces, my children! I am here, ready to pour out graces because I am your Mama who loves you so very, very much! **If you knew my love for you, you would not leave me, you would always be close to me. You would ask me for many graces with great faith because I do not abandon you, my children! It is you who abandon me, you who do not ask me for graces with faith.**

I want you all saints, my children, all saints. Give me all your heart, your love, and a great confidence in me.

My children, I cover you with graces, blessings, minute by minute; but you do not understand the graces I pour upon you. **So many persons have seen me and so many persons do not want to recognize Me!**

**I pour out such numerous graces on this little corner of the earth, many, many graces! But you are afraid to announce them! You tremble! Why? Why do you tremble whereas it is I who comes to save you?**

**Announce clearly that it is I who comes. Many persons have seen me. Many persons have received graces. Why are they not announced publicly? . . . Because the Faith diminishes!**

**It is Faith, my children: with Faith, one can move mountains and without Faith, one goes to hell. Ask for Faith! Ask for Faith, my children!**

36

Faith is a great grace, my children! I pardon everyone, the good and the wicked as well; one day, they will come to recognize who I am.

And here, I want a great Sanctuary: I want all my children. There are so many, many starving children! All of you should bring them many things, many . . . for the poor, for all.

Do you see this wind (blowing)? My children, this wind signifies all the graces that I pour on the whole world in this hour: great, great graces. One day, you will understand.

Be strong, be strong, my children! Do not fear, for I am here in your presence! **I will come soon to give you a great sign of love, of recognition, of affection. I will come to bring joy into your heart and into all hearts, the love of Jesus.**

Prepare yourselves to make a good Confession and a good Communion. Prepare yourselves, my children, do not wait until there is no more time. Prepare your soul with sincerity and Jesus will come to bring you many graces and many gifts. He will bring peace, harmony, serenity into your family. There is so little of this!

Ask for a great spiritual grace. I give you a strong blessing, that it assist you in your life and even more, at the moment of your death. I will send you many graces and much help the length of your journey and you will be in the grace of God and the Saints.

I am the Mama of all and I love you so very, very much, my children! I want you to love me. I can be loved by all, the good and the wicked as well. I want all to resurrect one day in Holy Paradise.

I bless you, my children, and hold you tightly in my arms. One day, I will come to take you in my arms and carry you away into the glory of Holy Paradise.

Pray! Pray! Do penance! **One day, I will come and give you a great Light and all will believe.**

I will give a great power to my 'instrument' that she may carry her heavy cross. Pray for her: that she may attain this glory that the Heavenly Mama has announced."

The Heavenly Mama gives her blessing.

## Message of the Most Blessed Virgin
### Friday, September 22, 1967

The narration of this Apparition together with Rosa's descriptions and prayers, alternating with the transmission of the Heavenly Mama's words clearly convey the unfolding of the Apparitions during the first years. One will note the accuracy and equilibrium of all that is said and described. Nothing is offensive or unusual, nor of a strangeness leading to nothing. The interventions of Heaven at San Damiano are steadfastly connected to the tradition of Faith and Christian prayer, to the Church, to her institutions and authority.

The prophetic announcement of a great Light in the sky will also be noted. The messages contain numerous prophecies, all interconnecting to affirm the coming of the Triumph of Mary and the New Reign of Jesus.

This message is very grave. The Virgin Mary looks at the world as it truly is, but she promises us victory even in the midst of the most terrible struggles if we remain closely united to her in Faith and prayer.

**Rosa:** "The Heavenly Mama is there with three Archangels and seven children robed in white; also Pope Pacelli with many deceased Bishops of Piacenza, all surrounding the Enclosure. They are wearing ceremonial robes, with the miter. The seven children are holding a book in one hand and a censer in the other."

**The Heavenly Mama:** "This signifies that all these souls came to accompany me here, in procession for me, to venerate me, to console me and they also pray very, very much for you, for the entire world, especially for those who are present here. They bless you (all who are present with the Madonna) and they pray."

**Rosa:** "She announces that Pope Pacelli is performing Saint Michael's exorcism. The seven children surround the Heavenly Mama, each with a rose lantern."

**The Heavenly Mama:** "My children, I call many souls into my Presence, many souls that I love, to unite themselves in prayer to save the world because the Eternal Father wants to do justice, my children, because you have not listened to the Heavenly Mama's supplications. I wait, I wait, I pray, I pray, I insist. But the Eternal Father wants to do justice.

Do you not understand what the chastisement signifies,

my children? You do not think, you do not reflect! You have already had so many wars and so much destruction! The world has been so destroyed! So many souls were lost! Do you not reflect on what would happen if there were a war now? I cry so very, very much, my children.

Why is it that I come always to call you? Do you not see that I am here in your presence, that I love you so, that I pour many graces on the world? The absent also receive graces from me, but they have drawn away from me, they insult me and make a laughingstock of me. Think, think, my children, that a Mother does everything for her children in order that they be saved. And you, my children, do not discourage me!

**One day, you will see a great Light in the sky which will pass everywhere and the whole world will see it.**

What will become of those who insulted me and made a laughingstock of me? What will be the state of their conscience when they present themselves before the Tribunal of God?

The graces I give you are diverse: conversions, cures of all sorts of sicknesses. I give light to all those who invoke me with faith. My children, revive your Faith! Revive your Faith, my children! Your Mama assists you. Revive your Faith and your great love for my Son Jesus. He will be merciful to you because Jesus is so merciful! He calls you, He waits for you and He wants your salvation, my children. I do so much to save you: I pass along the streets, along the roads, into homes, into villages, in cities and in all places to save you."

**Rosa:** (After an interval of silence.) "Yes, Mama, we promise you with all our heart. Give us much faith, give us much love! You know everything, Mama! Have pity on us. Be merciful, listen to our supplications! Do not abandon us and also those who do not pray in this terrible hour."

**The Heavenly Mama:** "Call many young people, my daughter! Call them all, night and day, especially during this novena to Saint Michael. Bring them all here in my Presence because I, with prayer, and the help of Saint Michael, (we) could do all. We could extract the grace of postponing the chastisements."

**Rosa:** "Yes, Mama, I promise this to you. Angels and Saints who are in Heaven, intercede also for us beside the

Heavenly Mama to obtain the grace of peace and also the grace to love her very much, with a great love and with sincere repentance.

The Heavenly Mama says that she can do everything, that she pours out many graces. The Heavenly Mama has a merciful smile on her lips."

Rosa then prays for the Pope, the bishops, the destitute, and for the whole world.

**The Heavenly Mama:** "Ask for graces. I extend my arms to give graces and blessings. I have in hand all kinds of roses, graces and blessings, my children. I so desire your good, a great love!"

The Heavenly Mama replies to various requests, especially to that of a priest asking for the cure of a thirty-six year old woman and for the conversion of another person.

"I will give you all that you ask. **Unite yourselves in prayer in church before Jesus exposed in the Blessed Sacrament. May all spouses do this because they must fight for Jesus and not for Satan. All must be reunited in peace, in the love of Jesus, not in discord, pride or vanity. Love, love, fraternal love, and love for me and for my Son Jesus!**

Pray! Pray, my children, to the Holy Spirit for the Church, for lost souls, in order that they may understand the evil they are doing. Pray! Pray! With my help, we will conquer. We must save them at any price because my Son Jesus died on the Cross to save all men. Come, let us unite ourselves in prayer, in sacrifices, with great love. We will be able to resolve everything and we will triumph in Heaven and also on earth.

I bless you, my children, I give you a strong blessing; that, with the help of your Guardian Angels, my sons of predilection (priests) may carry it to the confines of the earth.

In the Name of the Father, the Son, and the Holy Spirit! Amen!"

# Message of the Most Blessed Virgin
April 5, 1968
- Feast of Our Lady of the Seven Sorrows -

This message is of extraordinary intensity and resounds as a great cry from beginning to end. A cry of sorrow which we will better understand by recalling that this was the Feast-day of Our Lady of the Seven Sorrows . . . and by considering the state of the world in this hour! A cry of anguish in the face of humanity's destiny. A cry of motherly love, wounded both by the death of her Only Son on the Cross and by the damnation of so many of her sons here below which renders in vain such a Passion. You will note the words filled with hope when speaking of the Judgment and the many words of consolation in the midst of so much sorrow. The Virgin Mary has never proclaimed her sorrow with such pangs, such realism and such immense love.

"My children, I have come to inflame your heart, to set it on fire, to ask pity and mercy for you and for the whole world.

Remain prepared! Remain in the state of penance (state´ in penitenza!) Ask pity! For my Son Jesus, all wounded and scourged, is dying on the gibbet. You then, offer your sorrows and pains.

I am here in your presence to call my sons to penance and prayer: the cry of a Mother who calls her sons, who does not want to lose them but who wants to clasp them in her arms and press them to her Heart.

I want them to rest upon my breast and listen to my words as Mother, who shouts! Who shouts! . . . Who weeps bitterly in seeing so many sons on the edge of the precipice! But they do not listen to my word. They do not see the many, many souls going to perdition. So many tragic events, so many appalling things, so much clamoring, so many offenses to my Son Jesus!

The hour has struck, my children! They do not listen to the word of a Mother who weeps so very, very much, seeing my sons of predilection (priests) who do not listen to my word. They are being lost in the world: all for vainglory, for pride, for greed: nothing but ambition! They no longer want to call me by the sweet name of Mother. But what will become of them when this sad hour comes when they will all be terror-stricken? They will no longer have the strength to raise their eyes towards Heaven and call me. They will no longer be capable because the Eternal Father wants to do justice.

The Eternal Father is the Father of Love. He is merciful. But now He has said: "Enough!" my children, "Enough! Because you do not listen to My Spouse: a Mother who weeps, who shouts for help to save her sons."

Pray, my children! Pray and do not abandon me! Cling to me and look towards me, in this place where I come so often to see my sons - and to see myself abandoned after having poured out many graces, after having given so much love, after the many conversions I have granted!

Of what value are material graces if after that the soul is lost? My Son Jesus died on the Cross. But He died on the Cross to save you, to save your soul and one day, bring you into the Heavenly Fatherland.

You do not understand the sacrifice I made along the sorrowful way of Calvary: step by step, to follow my Son Jesus, to save my sons. I gave all of myself. I gave my Son, crucified, to save all humanity. But few understand the shout of a Mother who remains terrified.

Pray, my sons! Pray! Call souls to prayer and penance. Do not abandon me! I will not abandon you even for a moment. And when this terrible hour comes and you call me, I will be at your side; with Jesus in your heart, you will be strong in combat and you will conquer all the temptations and all the battles.

Do you not see so many of the young people in pride and arrogance? What lacerations they cause, trampling upon my Son Jesus with blasphemies and insults! Pray for those who offend Him. Pray, in order that they be converted, that they repent of their sins and that the Eternal Father gives them the kiss of pardon.

**I can do no more, my sons! I can no longer extend my arms and embrace you! The Father has said: 'Enough!' Now, He has left the whole world free. The devil will act! I weep so very much! I have suffered much with love and sorrow to save humanity! And now, to see it going to perdition!**

Suffer, and offer, my children, with me. Cling tightly to me! Do not abandon my place! It will be the place of refuge, the place of love, of tranquility, goodness, sweetness, where I will cover you with my mantle and clasp you in my arms.

Announce to everyone that they must pray. They must not abandon me and I will not abandon them. Do not wait until the sad hours arrive! If you are with me, you will conquer.

Continue in recollection. Keep yourselves tightly under my mantle with the Crown of the Rosary* in your hands. Recite it often and ask pity and mercy for all. Jesus, my Son, suffers so much! He is all lacerated. (* The entire Rosary, fifteen decades.)

My children, listen to me! Listen to my motherly call! Tell everyone not to abandon my place. That they strengthen themselves more in faith and love towards me. That they accept the cross and remain beside me; and we will triumph in all and through all.

I will place much joy in your heart and you will have the strength to carry the cross. I will give you much love for me and for my Son Jesus. I will give you much tranquility, much serenity, and you will be able to confront all that will come. For I am the Mama of Mercy and Pardon, the Co-Redemptrix of all, the salvation of all, who loves you so very much, my children, and wants to be loved by all my sons.

Blessed are those who will understand the love of a Mother!

I will place Saint Michael the Archangel close to you, your Guardian Angel, your Holy Defender, your Saint whose name you bear. They will not abandon you. They will help you during all the hours of the day, during all the hours of the night. But keep yourselves prepared, with Jesus in your heart: He will be your support.

When this hour comes when the Heavenly Mama will open the gates of Paradise for you, you will see with your own eyes the brilliant light of love of your Heavenly Mama, you will be so happy!

Blessed are those who will have suffered with me and with my Son Jesus! Let us suffer, let us weep, all united in one single heart!

Call souls! Call them, my children! Tell them not to abandon my place! That they listen to no one. That they come only to pray and to love me, in this place where they will find the joy and love of a Mother. I repeat this to you, my children! I announce this to you, my children! Listen to me! Each day, I wait so many hours for you! I am close to you so many hours of the night, to prepare you, to give you love and strength to conquer all the battles. My children, pray! Write! Telephone! Do not lose courage! Accept everything for love of my Son and your Heavenly Mama with an elan of love, with a smile on your lips, even at the cost of a sacrifice. You will have much merit above in Heaven!

When this hour comes when you must leave this earth, you will be surrounded by the Angels and Saints and your Heavenly Mama will present you before the Judge. He will embrace you and clasp you to Him and give you the kiss of love. You will enter into Paradise, glorious and triumphant, if you have been prompt to suffer, whatever the cost.

My children, put my words into practice! Place them in your mind and in your heart! That they be imprinted there as the seal of goodness and mercy of your Heavenly Mama.

My children, I enclose all of you in my Heart to make but one single heart with me.

**Do not fear, I will come in Triumph! I will come to give light, to enlighten souls. But it will be too late for those who no longer understand the love of a Mother. They will be in the midst of a terrible ordeal. The heavens and the earth will break loose and they will no longer be capable of raising their eyes to Heaven to implore pity and mercy.**

Pray! Pray, my children, all around my Paradise of this earth. Pray, and call me hour by hour, day by day. Do not tire of coming. Offer! Suffer! Endure! You will always have joy in your heart, the joy that your Mama will give you.

I bless you, my children, and I hold you tightly under my mantle, up to the moment when I will have you with me in Heaven. I repeat this to you; goodbye, my children! Until we meet again around this little flowered tree, blooming with flowers of purity!

The moment of purification will come when you will be purified, when I will come to embrace you anew. This will be the ultimate hour! I will bring you into the joy of Paradise.

Pray! Pray for everyone, even your enemies, even those who offend me: those who do not want to see me, those who do not want to love me, pray for them and then you will always have joy in your heart.

In the Name of the Father, and of the Son, and of the Holy Spirit! Amen!"

## Message of the Most Blessed Virgin
### December 20, 1968

This message is filled with both sorrow and love. While it recalls sin, it also recalls the tenderness of Jesus and it announces anew the Triumph of the Church and the Triumph of the Sorrowful Heart of Mary .

The Virgin Mary looks at and shows us the sin of the world on this December 20, vigil of a Feast and during a period which should celebrate the Innocence and Love of the Infant Jesus but which to the contrary, is the occasion for so much luxury, sins and sacrileges. Jesus-Love is forgotten.

The loss of souls, redeemed at so great a price, is brought to mind in this message. The Virgin Mary speaks to us at length of the Holy Father, Pope Paul VI, and the Church. She speaks to us again of Jesus, of His Gospel, of His Love; she tells of her work of salvation for Her children here below. Finally, as always, she finishes by addressing words of affection and encouragement.

"What sadness, what day of tears, to see so many souls being lost! Jesus died on the Cross to save you! He shed all His Blood. He is all Love! He gave His Body and His Blood to save souls. But few listen to Him! Few follow Him!

Pray! Pray! Pray! For the hours are sad, especially for my son, Paul VI, who is in the midst of a struggle filled with anguish and tears. Pray very much for him. Make a sacrifice in order that he has the strength and courage to embark in the world to give Faith and to speak clearly to all: that the Holy Spirit illuminates his mind and inflames his heart, that it may burn only with love for Jesus. Jesus is always with him. Jesus lives with him  night and day in suffering and in tears. Why do you not listen to him? Why do you not listen to his counsels? He who listens to him, listens to me. He who follows him, follows me. He who threatens him, threatens me.

Do you not know, my sons, that Jesus has always conquered and will always conquer? There will be struggles, there will be persecution, there will be diseases, everything. But the Church of Peter will triumph always, forever and ever.

Do you not read the Gospel? Do you not reflect on the Gospel? What Jesus said when He was on earth . . . How He spoke to souls. Jesus awaits you with so much anxiety! He awaits you at His feet. He wants to pardon. He wants to embrace you. He wants a mutual outpouring of hearts in an exchange of love, in faith, in sincerity, and in humility. He does not want pride, nor vainglory, nor malice. Malice leads to hell. Jesus reigns and Jesus will reign for all eternity.

**Pray, and have hours of Adoration to postpone all the chastisements that the Eternal Father wants to send. Reunite yourselves by groups in reciting the Rosary to ask pity and mercy.**

I am the Mama of Love. I am the Mama of Consolation. I am the Queen of Heaven and earth. I am the Mother of the Universe, the Dispensatrix of graces. I call, I call my sons around me to cover them with graces, love and consolation.

Do, undo, and re-do all that you can, but my power, my assistance, my Sorrowful Heart will triumph in the entire world. I want to save my sons! I want to love my sons! I want to bring my sons to Heaven with me! Forward! Forward! Forward, my sons!

I let fall many roses with thorns but I also let fall many roses without thorns which will be so perfumed that they will always raise you more to sanctity, to love for me.

Do not fear, my sons! Pray! Pray! Pray! Everything is obtained through prayer. Do not grow weary of praying night and day. Under my mantle, you will have everything and you will know everything. I will inspire you. I will assist you. I will guide you along your way of life, to have you above with me one day.

Accept everything through love for me. Offer everything through love for me. If you are trampled upon but your soul is innocent, your soul flies to Heaven triumphant. Only prayer will make you strong, only Faith triumphs, and only my powerful hand guides you step by step to sanctity.

Courage, my sons! Jesus is with you. Your Heavenly Mama is beside you covering you with her mantle. I hold you tightly in my arms so that you will never leave me again.

I send you a strong blessing, in the Name of the Eternal Father, in the Name of the Son, in the Name of the Holy Spirit! Amen. Until we meet again, my children, always under my mantle!"

## Message of the Most Blessed Virgin
October 26, 1969
- Feast of Christ the King -

This message denotes the Feast celebrated on that day, that of Christ the King. Jesus is present; the Madonna declares this at the beginning.

We find again the great themes of the messages: the young, the consecrated, the Faith, the Merciful Love of Jesus, the Eucharist. But always, new words help us to discover even more concerning these realities. And those of this message are grave and beautiful.

The words concerning Pope Paul VI and the obedience due him will most certainly be noted, as also those words concerning the Church of Peter as Jesus founded it. We read such a message with wonder, for it contains so much wisdom and so much love that it alone would suffice to manifest the truth of the Apparitions of San Damiano.

"My children, I have returned among you with my Son Jesus Who is the King of kings, to bring you peace and love, to enter into your heart and to be the center of love of your heart. The King of kings wants to inflame all your hearts with love for Him. Cling to Him, my children, cling to Him, for Jesus can give you everything and He loves you so!

He calls all the apostles of the world to go and preach the truth, Faith, love and pardon. He calls all the young to Christian love, to purity, to humility. For purity is a great gift! Be pure! Be humble! And you will enter into the Kingdom of Heaven.

Jesus is with you. Jesus wants to reign with you. Jesus wants to pour graces and mercy on the world.

Pray! Intensify your prayers; offer and forgive, and you will be forgiven. All unite to Him, especially in the Holy Eucharist; He will set your heart afire and thus destroy all sins. He will inflame it only with love and will purify it.

Give all of yourselves to Him, give all your sins and you will be forgiven. Send Him a kiss of love and He will render you an even stronger love. Forward! Always with Jesus! Never sin again, but love Him very much because He died on the Cross for you. He wants to live only to love you so that one day, you will come to re-find Him above in Heaven.

My children, listen to me, listen to me, for the moments are so sad! Pray with more fervor, with more love. Jesus will forgive you, Jesus will listen to your prayers. Because on this earth . . . everything passes, but eternity, never! There, you will revel in eternal happiness.

Pray! Pray! Pray! Pray for the Holy Father, Pope Paul VI, for all the Church: **that the Church of Peter triumphs such as Jesus founded it. Peter must be the Head of the Church; you must listen to the Holy Father. You must love him. You must obey him. Pray for him and Jesus will give him strength, courage to put the truth of the Faith into practice which must be strong.**

My children, I want all of you under my mantle and under the mantle of my Son Jesus, Who is all love. Come! Adore Him! Love Him! Jesus is the King of kings, the King of the strong. Jesus is meek and humble of Heart. He calls all my children of the world to humility, to sanctity. Live with love for Him alone. Do not preoccupy yourselves so with material things, but preoccupy yourselves with saving your soul. Re-enter into grace with God and you will understand many things. Think! And reflect!

I am the Mother of the Church. I am the Queen of Apostles. May all my apostles be holy, for great is their mission of sanctity, of goodness, of charity and of pardon. May all these sons unite! May all these sons love one another with the love of Jesus!

Come, and do not delay!

In the Name of my Son Jesus, I give you a strong blessing which assists you in life and in death.

In the Name of the Father, and of the Son, and of the Holy Spirit! Amen!"

Rosa adds: "The consecrated must bless with Jesus, your Brother, says the Mama."

"In the Name of the Father, and of the Son, and of the Holy Spirit! Amen!

"Sing Christus Vincit!"

## Message of the Most Blessed Virgin
May 2, 1970
- First Saturday of the Month -

Moved by the reflection that very soon this voice would no longer be heard, we read this message with emotion because it is so deeply imprinted with tenderness. The message of May 31, 1970, while not the last message, was the last one to be publicly transmitted.

We also again find here the intentions which are dear to the Heavenly Mama: before everything, the salvation of souls, eternal salvation. This expression is found repeatedly . . . as a continued resounding of the beatings of her Immaculate Heart. If we welcome, if we accept these very simple words, mysterious in their simplicity, of this mystery of love that reaches the hearts of the children of God, we feel so very close to the Virgin! One would certainly have to hear them as they were pronounced by Rosa, marked by the sentiments of the Madonna. These are a Mother's words of love, an effusion of her solicitude; they are also of a language that reflects her firm determination to save her children at any price.

"My children who surround me, kneeling at my feet and under my mantle, I am here among you. I inspired your mind. I have called you to prayer, to penance, because I want to give you testimony of much love and I want to know the love you have for me because I love you so very, very much!

I want to give you numerous graces. I will convert many souls and will strew along your way, graces, mercy, pardon, resignation to carry the cross.

You must not fear when you have the cross because you have Jesus at your side Who assists you, consoles you, gives you strength to surmount every obstacle to carry the cross with Him, and to purify souls, to cure them soul and body.

If they are prepared for Heaven, Jesus gives the strength, the support to rejoin Him: through purification on earth, they enter into the glory of Heaven.

Think, my children, think what a day of happiness today is, to be united to all my children in love. What joy you give me, you who have listened to my invitation of Mother, of Queen and Refuge of sinners, Consolation of the afflicted . . . (and, with sweetness and tenderness,) I am the Mother of all and I love you so! I would like to see all of you in Heaven with me one day!

I call everyone: the poor, the rich, the young, the old, all united to me. And one day, you will understand why I called you, why I came in this place. For there is so much mire in the world! They think of advancing only through science but science is of little use for eternity. The corporal and spiritual works of mercy are needed for eternity; humility is needed, poverty and purity are needed, and charity, to live in a Christian manner; and to persevere until death, as Jesus wants. He died on the Cross for you, to save you, to purify you with His Blood.

Jesus is risen; you, also, will rise one day. When the hour of departure from this earth comes for each one of you, if you are called for eternity, if you are prepared, if you have called me, and you have listened to my invitation, I will come and take you with much joy and bring you before my Son Jesus. I will be your Advocate, with Saint Michael, with your Guardian Angel, and we will assist you always, where you must go, wherever your destination . . . But one day, you will enter into glory!

Forward! Forward, my children! Close to me, live only with love for me and for my Son Jesus. I assist you step by step.

I have covered the sky with my mantle to cover all of you, the good and the wicked as well. I want to save you! That is why I come, my children, I want to save you! I want to enlighten you so that you may understand that you must repent and revive the Faith and love for my Son and for me.

This is what I ask of you, starting with *tomorrow:* that it be a day for the Holy Father, Paul VI, who is on the Cross with Jesus. As Jesus arose, he also will rise one day.

*Monday* - that it be for the holy souls in Purgatory; for the consecrated, nuns, and for everyone. Pray!

*Tuesday* - that it be only for the young: that they flower in the love for Jesus and for me; that they understand how much I love them and how much Jesus loves them.

*Wednesday* - that it be for all the families of the world, that they may imitate my Patriarch, Saint Joseph, in humility, in love and in silence.

*Thursday* - that it be only to adore and thank Eucharistic Jesus.

*Friday* - that it be for all the consecrated of the

world.

*And Saturday* - for the conversion of all sinners; that they all return repentant, in my Heart. That they may ask pardon and receive pardon before the sad hours arrive.

Offer this during this month.

I will always be with you. Live always with me, in joy, in love, with Jesus.

Always receive Jesus in your heart, and knock! Knock! Ask for graces! All will be granted you.

Open your arms and lift your eyes to Heaven, my children! Lift your eyes toward Heaven where I await you one day. Ask pity and mercy for my mercy is great towards my children.

Progress always more in the good, with Christ, through Christ, and in Christ.

Offer your day in the morning in union with Jesus and with me and you will be assisted all during the day and all during the night. Your Guardian Angel will follow you step by step and will enlighten you to walk in the way of good. The Holy Spirit will enlighten you and will give you much love.

Unite yourselves constantly to the Choirs of Angels to adore and thank Jesus and to make reparation to Him for the many offenses, the many sacrileges. Promise to love Him very much. One day, you will understand so many things! I will inspire you.

**Do not fear. Always revive the Faith even more, for my Triumph will come. Yes, it will come! All will see it and all will understand what I have announced to save you.**

Unite yourselves day after day at my feet and do not tire of prayer; you will have much happiness and consolation in your heart!

In the Name of my Son Jesus, I give you a strong blessing which assists you in life and in death, with the Angels and with the Saints.

In the Name of the Father, and of the Son, and of the Holy Spirit! Amen!

Always united to me in one single heart! I love you and desire that you always be near me, Queen of Heaven and Mother of the Universe, who loves you so."

Rosa announces that the Heavenly Mama will bless all

the buses and cars and asks all to recite three Ave Marias. She signals that in this moment, the Virgin is at the back of the field and asks priests to turn in this direction to bless.

### The Messages of Jesus

Following are three messages given by Jesus. We make no comments prior to their presentation for they are of a gravity, a beauty, a mercy, worthy of the Son of God, made Man.

### Message given by Jesus
October 27, 1968
- Feast of Christ the King -

"My brothers, I am here among you to give you much joy, I, Who am the King of kings. I am the Mercy for all, I give pardon to all. But I want you to place yourselves in accord with Me. I want to save all of you.

My children, open your heart with Me, open it! All your thoughts, your desires, your misfortunes, your sorrows, your joys; tell Me everything so I can comfort you, support and protect you, I, Who am the King of the Universe, the King of all, Who can give peace to all, in hearts and in nations, for Jesus has always conquered, and He will conquer always.

**The Heart of My Mama will Triumph and My Reign will come in the entire world. If you listen, you will have an abundance of graces, but if you do not listen to My word, great chastisements will come; they will pounce upon you!**

"That is sufficient," the Eternal Father has said. "That is enough!" Why do you want to travel through the ways of sin? I have given you so much intelligence, science, knowledge! I have filled you with these! But the more intelligence you have, the more you listen to the devil and travel the way of perdition!

Be humble! Be poor! Be gentle and benevolent! Do as I when I was on this earth, beside My Mama, beside My Adopted father: I listened to their counsels and I loved them so, always in poverty, always in humility, always in clemency.

Why do you preoccupy yourselves so, doing, talking,

52

having? Everything passes in this world! I put you on this earth in order that you prepare yourselves for Heaven. It is there that I await you, there, where you will revel in eternal felicity. I think of it day by day! You should leave everything. You should take care of your soul: that it be innocent! When you will present yourselves at the Tribunal and I will be there in your presence, what will you be able to tell Me?

Reflect, My children! Reflect, My brothers, while you are still in this time when I welcome you with love! I welcome you with great joy, if you are prepared. I pardon you. I have mercy. I give you everything! It is up to you to repent! It is up to you to ask mercy! Prepare your heart! Prepare your soul!

Do not preoccupy yourselves so with material affairs! Time passes quickly! And death approaches! The chastisements are drawing near! Reflect! Reflect! I pardon. I have mercy.

I bless all of you, those who are near and those who are far away. I give you love. I give you mercy. I give you pardon.

In the Name of the Father, and of the Son, and of the Holy Spirit!"

**Message given by Jesus**
March 6, 1970
- First Friday of the Month -

After the Virgin says a few words, Jesus speaks. Then the Madonna gives a message following that of Jesus. It is reproduced in part:

**The Most Blessed Virgin:** "My children, I am here with my Son Jesus, Who is the King of kings."

**Jesus:** "I am the Good Shepherd, Who comes to save My sheep, to bring them into the Father's House, to give them all My love, to give them all My mercy, for I want to save My brothers, I want to save them! I do not want them to be lost.

Come! Come to Me! I will comfort you. Come to Me! I will purify you! Come to Me! I will sanctify you! I am Master. I am Judge. I am Merciful. I want to save all My Mother's children who are here below.

My Mother comes to help you, to save you, to give you a word of comfort and consolation. Listen to her! Listen to her! While there is still time! **Listen to My Heavenly Mama and yours! Listen to her! The Eternal Father sends her in this place. Think and reflect!**

I am Jesus, all torn by the grave sins which humanity commits, by the many sacrileges, because they no longer listen to their Brother. I want to be with you, My brothers! I want to inflame your heart, and I want to reign in your hearts. For I gave all My Blood to purify you, to make you pure, so that you could arrive in Heaven beside Me, beside My Mama and yours.

Ask pardon! Ask mercy! Ask for a great Faith! It is Faith which brings one to Heaven. It is Faith which surmounts all obstacles. Be firm!

**My Mama will come to give you a great Light, be it in peace or be it in the storm. She has repeated this to you so many times!**

Why do you not listen to a Mama who gives you all the graces, who calls you to penance to save you? Think! Think, My brothers!

Look at the world, how it is marching toward the abyss! So much mire! So much calumny! So much pride! So much malice! Pray. Offer. Suffer. And be silent. My Mama and yours will do everything."

**The Most Blessed Virgin:** "I am the Queen of Heaven, the Mother of the Universe, who loves you so! I want all of you under my mantle . . .

So many of the dying leave this earth with no one to assist them, with no one to give them one word of comfort! They depart in anguish. Their heart is transpierced. They have no word of comfort, of light, or preparation for death, from earth to Heaven. What sorrow! Pray! Pray, my children, for the dying! Bring them a word of comfort, of resignation. You will be assisted. The souls of Purgatory do so much for you . . "

**Message given by Jesus**
March 26, 1970
- Holy Thursday -

The message given on this day was spoken entirely by

Jesus. You will note the titles which belong to Christ-Jesus.

"I am Jesus. I am **your Brother,** Who calls you to My Heavenly Table, to enrich you with graces and pardon. Reunite yourselves, reunite yourselves at My Table! And I will ask pity and mercy of the Eternal Father. I will give you many graces. I will give you much comfort. But2.188 have a firm Faith, with love for Me, My children.

For I am the **King of kings.** I am full of mercy. Do you not see how much I suffer for you? Unceasingly, I ask mercy of My Heavenly Father: That He pardon you! That you may all return repentant, so that you may come into My arms one day, above in Heaven where I await you!

I am Jesus, the **Savior of the world.** I come to save you. Listen to Me! Listen to Me! For My mercy is great. I can do everything, beside My Heavenly Father. Do not fear in the struggles! Be strong, as I was when I walked along the way of Calvary.

Ask the Eternal Father: 'May Your Will be done and not mine!', as I Myself asked Him. Then you will find everything: strength, courage, love. You will understand so many things! For I give you everything, that which you ask; but above all, I give you My love, because My love is great when it penetrates within you. My love is strong in your heart. I want to beat in your heart. I want to give so many graces!

May the Holy Spirit enlighten you with His love! That you may understand that My Mama and yours comes to save you, that My Mama suffers much for you! And suffered much at the foot of the Cross, when I was dying on the Cross! That My Blood purifies you and sanctifies you for Heaven!

I am the **Living Jesus.** I want to enter into your heart to inflame it. I want to enrich it with graces: spiritual and temporal graces. Come! Come to the Eucharistic Banquet! Come, and do not delay! I will pardon you.

Make a good examination of conscience. Prepare your heart, pure as snow, and I will enter into your heart. I will enlighten your mind, I will inflame your heart with much love.

Do not think so much of the things of the world! Everything ends! I put you on this earth so that you would come anew into My arms above, where I await you with so much love! Everything passes here below! Everything passes!

**If you listen, I, beside My Heavenly Father, will lessen the chastisements.**

If you listen to My Mama and yours, she will do so much for you! And she does so much, day and night! She comes on this earth, My Mama and yours, at dawn of day, to walk in this world, to enlighten all her children, to bless them, and to give them an abundance of help and comfort.

Come, and do not delay! You will understand everything, and you will have everything! I bless you and hold you tightly in My loving arms.

In the Name of the Father, and of the Son, and of the Holy Spirit! Amen!"

### Message of Saint Michael the Archangel
September 29, 1968
- Feast of Saint Michael -

"I am Saint Michael. I am your brother, who loves you so and wants to defend you against all the dangers of soul and body, against temptations and against all evil.

I am always here with you. I watch night and day with you. My wings are greater than all the doves, in the heavens and on earth, and also on the ocean; on ships and in all parts of the world where they have recourse to me.

This day, the Heavenly Mama has given me many graces to give to all! She has given me comfort to bestow, and more strength to battle against the enemy.

Many persons are present here who fight against me and against the Mama of Heaven! But we fear no one because the Heavenly Mama, with her power and I, with my sword, will crush the head of the enemy and we will free many souls troubled by grave sins.

Pray! Pray together, my brothers! With prayer and with sacrifice, we will conquer all. We will unfurl all the banners of Love, Peace, Charity and Purity.

I have asked the Heavenly Mama to pardon all those who in this day are in the grace of God or are placing themselves therein.

Forward! Forward with Christ! Forward! Forward with our Mama of Heaven who will triumph over the entire world and gain victory.

I am the Prince of Heaven who renders honor to the

Queen of Heaven and Mother of the Universe, who so loves her sons here below!

All the Angels and Archangels, especially, are holding a great feast in my honor. They help me in battle to save souls, to save my brothers and the young people, young such as I, whom I love so! I surround them with love.

How happy you made me yesterday, to see so many of the young surrounding the Heavenly Mama's Garden! I passed all around the Garden with my sword and I defended the young against dangers and temptations. They were all love and all joy. But promise, my brothers, to be always thus during your whole life and you will greatly console those who are dear to you, and your Heavenly Mama, who does everything to give you graces and to give you much love.

Forward! Forward, young people! With Jesus in your heart, we must conquer! But conquer with Jesus, not with Satan, because Satan brings you to perdition.

Let not your mind be troubled. You must always be serene. Call me often and I will always defend you with my sword.

I go throughout the world. I transport the Heavenly Mama from one place to another, with the Angels and Archangels, to help and console you.

**Come! Come, young people, in this place where you will find everything: material and spiritual graces and the grace to arrive in Heaven one day.**

I am Saint Michael the Archangel, he to whom the Eternal Father has given so much power to go throughout the world to free souls and save them. You must be strong! Pray! Pray with the Rosary which is the most powerful weapon to receive everything. You, with the Rosary, and I with my sword, will conquer everything and we will have everything: so much joy and so much love!

The Mama of Heaven has called you in this place today to reunite all hearts, near and far. With prayer, through the intermediary of the Guardian Angel and with my help, we will console all the brothers of the world, especially those who are in prison, innocent: those who are in concentration camps, who suffer so much! There are very, very many who are suffering the agony of Jesus: martyrdom! But Jesus is with them, Jesus sustains them and I defend them in so many things with my sword!

Let us pray! Let us pray! That it be only a day of prayer, songs and love. That all our hearts be united in the Heart of Jesus and in our Heavenly Mama's.

Forward! Forward, my brothers! **Let us all fight for the Glory of God, for the salvation of the Church; for the Church of Peter must reign until the end of time.** Jesus has always reigned and will reign always, in all hearts and everywhere. Jesus is with you and I am beside you, who gives you many inspirations and strengthens you even more in the Faith, to save you and bring you to Heaven one day with me."

# CHAPTER 4

## PROPHETIC ANNOUNCEMENTS

Prophecies have always existed in the history of the Church. We know those of the Old Testament. We know that the New Testament, the Gospel and the Apocalypse in particular equally announce the coming of the Church and of Humanity. The Acts of the Apostles contain several more immediate prophecies concerning the mission of the Apostles. Saint Paul himself attests to the existence of prophecies in the bosom of Christian communities: "Do not scorn the prophecies."

Numerous prophecies, be they of brief or long duration, took place during the lives of the Saints. Saint Grignon de Montfort can probably be considered as one of the prophets of the latter times. Among the great recent prophecies, we can mention those given at La Salette. And we know that very grave prophecies were given at Fatima.

At San Damiano, the Most Blessed Virgin Mary has announced five principal events, or an ensemble of events, which can be grouped under the following titles: the Coming of San Damiano; the Chastisements; the Great Light which will be given in the world; the Triumph of Mary; the New Reign of Jesus.

It must be noted that nowhere does there exist a chronology of these events. Must we speak of the Coming of San Damiano before speaking of the Chastisements? The messages do not respond to this question; therefore, do not consider the arrangement of this chapter a precise program of the announced prophecies. On the other hand, the Great Light and the Triumph of Mary are often associated in the messages. In the meantime, for the sake of greater clarity, we will speak very distinctly.

It will be observed that almost all of these announcements are announcements of hope. One must meditate at great length upon San Damiano and reflect on these words that are forever new, in a language that is always simple. Blessed are those who will grasp the treasure of Hope contained in the Virgin Mary's words!

**The Coming of San Damiano**   "Here, I want a
                                 great Sanctuary. I
                                 want all my children."
                                 (August 15, 1966)

The Madonna made four prophetic announcements concerning the coming of San Damiano.

First of all, the Virgin Mary asks for and announces the future realization of a great Sanctuary in this place, a Sanctuary which will be very, very great and which must welcome pilgrims who will flock here from the entire world: "That all may come from all parts of the world to ask for graces." (August 20, 1965) This Sanctuary must have fifteen altars in honor of the fifteen Mysteries of the Rosary: "Remember, my children, that I want a great, great Sanctuary, with fifteen altars." (August 12, 1966) Mama Rosa specified that high above the Sanctuary must be a statue of the Virgin of Loreto. Lamps in the forms of roses and stars must shine under the cupola of the Sanctuary.

The Heavenly Mama announces the triumph of this place of graces: "One day, this place will rise triumphant." (November 17, 1967) "A day will come when the bells of San Damiano will ring in celebration." (March 25, 1968) Let us not forget that the Madonna's Triumph depends on us: by our prayers, our fidelity to the Virgin's call and in giving testimony of the very numerous graces received, as she has so often asked.

More precisely, the Virgin Mary announces that this place will become an International Center of the entire world. She announces this solemnly, adding this Will of astonishing import: this must be the greatest Sanctuary in the whole world -

**"The whole world will come here at my feet, from all nations. I want an International Center of the entire world. All will come and prostrate themselves in prayer. I promised this to my 'instrument' the first day I came. I announced that the whole world would come here at my feet, that I want an International Center of the entire world under the title of 'Roses': the greatest Sanctuary in the world!"** (March 25, 1968)

Jesus also has announced His Will that it be so

done:

"... That they may recognize that the Heavenly Mama is in this Enclosure; this will become the International Center of My Heavenly Mama." (December 1, 1967)

The Madonna thinks of helping her children in every manner. She wants homes "in which to place the numerous homeless children." (December 8, 1966) She wants us to think of all the corporal and spiritual necessities. (This will be discussed in a special chapter at the end of this book.)

## The Chastisements

"Do you not see the chastisements occurring in all parts of the world?" (December 1, 1967)

"I have come on this earth to bring peace in hearts and in nations, and they have not accepted it." (May 25, 1967)

The Madonna's words bring to mind those of Jesus, weeping over Jerusalem: "Jerusalem, Jerusalem! you who kill the prophets, and stone those who are sent to you! How often would I have gathered your children together, as a hen gathers her young under her wings, but you would not!" (Saint Matthew, Ch. 23, v. 37)

"And when He drew near and saw the city, He wept over it, saying, "If you had known, in this your day, even you, the things that are for your peace! . . . because you have not known the time of your visitation!" (Saint Luke Ch. 19, v. 42, 44)

"The hour has struck! The hour has struck! The Eternal Father no longer temporizes!" (August, 1967)

With infinite sadness, the Virgin Mary announces terrible chastisements for humanity as a consequence of sin and because her motherly word has not been accepted. The chastisements will be terrible; they are imminent and are being held back only through the fervent prayer and penance of some of the faithful.

After reflecting, one can understand that these chastisements are inevitable. We must adore the patience of God Who endures so many sacrileges and so many crimes in granting sinners the time for repentance. The Madonna clearly indicates: "Jesus is merciful. He waits. He waits to see what you do. But afterwards, chastisements will pounce heavily upon humanity: chastisements of all kinds! Why do you not listen to your Heavenly Mama who loves you so?"

The Heavenly Mama speaks of chastisements in almost every message but she has given no detailed descriptions of them at San Damiano. She has done so elsewhere. At San Damiano, she insists above all on the cause of the chastisements and also on their consequences: that when they arrive, men will no longer be able to get up. We must be converted now and ask pardon. However, the Divine Mercy will always be open for whoever asks pity and mercy, even at the final moment:

**"Do you not see that the world is rushing forward into the abyss and destruction? I have been announcing these chastisements to you for a long time. They will become heavier if you do not listen to my motherly word. The Eternal Father is weary!"** (May 30, 1968) **"When you see the fire and the whole world burning, what will become of you who do not listen to my motherly word?"** (March 22, 1968) **"When this terrible chastisement comes, what will become of them if they have not believed? There will no longer be time to wake up."** (December 22, 1967)

These are infinitely sad words for a Mother who let her Son Jesus die to save humanity! "I have suffered so with love and sorrow to save humanity! And now, to see it going to perdition!" (April 5, 1968) "You do not understand the sacrifice I made along the sorrowful Way of Calvary: step by step, to follow my Son Jesus, to save my sons! I gave all of myself. I gave my Son, crucified, to save all humanity. But few understand the shout of a Mother who remains terrified." (April 5, 1968)

The great sin for which the Eternal Father reproaches humanity is that of not listening to the Heavenly Mama who comes with such love to convince her children to repent, who comes to console them, to save and pardon them, to love them. This is the supreme grace of mercy at the hour when humanity has already merited the scourge one hundred times over! And to still close our eyes to our sins and send away the Mama whose Heart is filled with mercy, who has nothing but words of love! . . And men trample upon her words! The Madonna has spoken of this in heartrending words: "The Eternal Father is the Father of Love. He is merciful. But now, He has said: 'Enough!' my children, 'Enough! Because you do not listen to My Spouse: A Mother who weeps, who shouts for help to save her sons!" (April 5, 1968)

## The Great Light

"You will never be able to understand the beauty, the grandeur, the goodness of the mercy of God."
(November 22, 1967)

All of God's works are imprinted with His Love, His Truth, His Justice, His Mercy, His Sweetness, His Tenderness, His Humility, with all His Infinite Perfections.

The chastisements themselves are a work of His Mercy. First of all, (1) because previously, God sent His Only Son here below to suffer death on the Cross, to save us; (2) because God defers and diminishes them, especially through the intercession of the Blessed Virgin Mary, with a compassion and patience we will not entirely understand even in Heaven; (3) because if there were a less severe way to save humanity, God would choose it; (4) because in the midst of these chastisements, God will look upon each gasp, each breath, with His Love of God, to grant mercy; (5) because through these chastisements, hearts so hardened that they would not have been saved by the Heavenly Mama's goodness will perhaps at times be saved, as rocks are broken when subjected to the hardest blows; (6) because, through these chastisements and the sufferings they involve, the elect will be purified and raised to a still greater glory; (7) because, through these chastisements, humanity will be delivered from evil, as we ask in the Our Father: "Deliver us from evil!"

The thoughts of God are "thoughts of peace and not of affliction" (twenty-third Sunday after Pentecost); "age after age, the thoughts of His Heart are to deliver their soul from death and to nourish them in their hunger" (Feast of the

Sacred Heart); "God is light and in Him there is no darkness." (First Epistle of Saint John, Ch. 1)

God is a continual effusion of Love and Light, of Mercy and Tenderness. This is His very Essence: "God is Love. And whoever lives in love, lives in God and God lives in Him." (Saint John, Ch. 4)

God wants to pour this effusion of Love and Light on the earth in these latter times as He did through the Birth of His Only Son on earth: through the Most Blessed Virgin Mary, she of whom it is said: "Lumen Aeternum, mondo effudit" - "She has communicated the Eternal Light to the world." (Preface of the Blessed Virgin Mary) It is she who, after having given the beneficial dew of Salvation by reason of the awaited Savior, will give in all hearts with tenderness and power the new rain prefigured by the prophet Elias, a rain which must re-generate hearts, according to what is written: "To all those who have received it, He has given the power of becoming children of God." (Saint John, Ch. 1)

However, this new effusion will not be like the first. Because the first time, as He said, Jesus was sent only to the lost sheep of the House of Israel whereas the Apostles had the mission, with the Church, of diffusing the Light in the world by preaching the Gospel and giving witness of their Faith, for as Saint Paul said: "How then, are they to call upon Him if they do not believe in Him? And how are they to believe without having heard Him? And how are they to hear, if no one preaches?" (Saint Paul to the Romans, Ch. 10)

This new effusion of Light announced by the Virgin Mary at San Damiano will be diffused this time in all consciences. It will penetrate all hearts, throwing them into confusion as It confused the conscience of Saint Paul, overwhelming and blinding him to all he had seen and known up until then. It will be diffused in the entire world, according to this passage from Holy Scripture: "It shines from East to West and there is no one who hides from His Ardor."

We can now turn to the Canticles which the Church places on our lips and which concern this Light, which enlightens all men who come into the world and which must shine in this extraordinary manner, a manner that the darkness cannot smother:

"Ornament your dwelling, Sion, and welcome Christ the

King. Open your arms to Mary, through whom Christ has come. For she brings the King of Glory, our New Light." (Liturgy of the Feast of the Purification of Mary.)

"I will come soon to give you Light: a strong Light, and many souls will be converted. I will place great joy, great Faith, in hearts, which will overcome all obstacles." (February 23, 1968)

"Soon, I will come, my children! Soon, I will be among you with a great Light. I will enlighten the entire world. Many souls will cry because they did not listen to my call." (February 23, 1968)

"Blessed are those who believe and hope in me for when I come with the Light, I will place much joy in their hearts; never before will they have experienced all the love I give to my sons." (June 21, 1968)

This Light will be given to the eyes and it will be given in hearts. It will be seen in the sky by the whole world and in the whole world. But at the same time, it will penetrate consciences as an irresistible sword, concerning which Jesus said to Saint Paul: "It is hard to kick against the goad." That is why no one will be able to resist the Light of God. Now, is the power of darkness. Then, will be the power of Light and it will be incomparable and supreme:

"But for those who insult me, those who do not believe, the Eternal Father will place such anguish in their hearts, such remorse and so many tears, that they will no longer have peace." (June 21, 1968)

"You will see one day: you will see a great Light in the sky which will pass everywhere. I will pass above everyone in a cloud and everyone will see me. What will become of those who insulted me and made a laughingstock of me? My poor sons, what will their conscience be when they present themselves before the Tribunal of God?" (September 22, 1967)

"I will come soon, my sons, to travel through the entire world. I will give a great sign in the sky for those who will still want to be saved. All those who have recourse to me, who have a look of repentance, this will be sufficient to save

**them."** (June 21, 1968)

**"I will come soon with a great Light to convert many souls. And then, the heavens and the earth will tremble by my power. Then all minds will be enlightened and all hearts will be set on fire with love for me."** (August 5, 1968)

**The Triumph of Mary**     Rosa announces
that a  great company of Angels
are here.  Each is holding a red
rose and a white  banner: "Long
live the Triumph of Mary!
Long live the Reign of
Jesus!"

The Triumph of Mary and the Reign of Jesus are constantly linked together in the announcements of the Blessed Virgin Mary at San Damiano. One time, Rosa saw these four letters  in the sky: **T M R J**, in the form of a cross; the first two letters were vertical, the last two horizontal.  The Madonna prescribed that Rosa  make little squares of material with the letters arranged on them as described.

The Triumph of Mary was announced in the Apocalypse. It has been announced by several enlightened souls, among them Saint Louis-Marie Grignon de Montfort.

This Triumph will be that of her Sorrowful and Immaculate Heart as she declared at Fatima. It will be the Triumph of Love, signified by the very beautiful words of the Madonna concerning the Great Light. But it is Mary who must triumph; it is her own Triumph which causes hell to tremble and the elect to rejoice. It is the Triumph of her who called herself a humble servant and whose humility confounded the Angels of Heaven. "He has regarded the humility of His handmaid; for behold, henceforth, all generations shall call me blessed. Because He that is mighty has done great things for me. And Holy is His Name."

**"I will come soon in great Triumph. I will awaken hearts. I will pardon all those who ask, who hope, who love."** (August 15, 1968)

**"I will come in my power, and I will open the heavens, the clouds. I will enlighten the whole**

66

world. Many souls will be converted and many souls will enter into Heaven. A great, great number will leave this earth.

Prepare yourselves, my children, for the hour approaches! If you have Jesus in your heart, Jesus will give you the strength, Jesus will give you the courage to enter into glory." (March 8, 1968)

As we see it, this will be a great and fearsome day. But the manifestation of the glory of the Virgin Mary will be all Love and Mercy. Those who will tremble in anguish will do so because of the darkness within them and not because of the Light coming from God, for "Mercy laughs at judgment." The Madonna will come to save "the little and the humble of the earth" and her Heart will reveal Itself to hearts. "I want my Heart to triumph in all hearts." (November 17, 1967) As Saint John said: "There is no fear in love," and "Whoever has this hope in Him is made pure, as He is pure." (First Epistle of Saint John Ch. 4:17 and 3:3.)

We will indeed see that one of the great reasons for the Virgin Mary's intervention at San Damiano is to prepare our hearts for her Triumph and for the Reign of Jesus.

"The day of my Triumph will come. You will sing with joy and gladness. There will be great joy and consolation in your hearts and those who did not believe will cry and suffer in anguish." (March 8, 1968)

"Prepare all hearts for my Coming!" (November 17, 1967)

THE NEW REIGN OF JESUS

"Jesus will return on this earth. His Reign will be one of mercy and pardon for all. Jesus will come with a great procession of Angels and Martyrs. He will go on all roads, everywhere." (December 29, 1967)

No one can form a proper notion of the Triumph of Mary and the Reign of Jesus. These events which will certainly be associated with the extraordinary manifestation of Divine Power on earth are of an Apocalyptic dimension. They are admirably united in the lesson contained in the liturgy for the Feast of the Apparitions of Our Lady of Lourdes:

"And the Temple of God in Heaven was opened, and there was seen the Ark of His Covenant in His Temple, and there came flashes of lightning and peals of thunder, and an earthquake, and great hail.

And a great sign appeared in heaven: a Woman clothed with the Sun, and the moon was under her feet, and upon her head a crown of twelve stars.

And I heard a loud voice in heaven saying: 'Now has come the Salvation, and the Power, and the Kingdom of our God and the Authority of His Christ'!" (Apocalypse, Ch. 11 and 12)

Let us remember that Ark of the Covenant is one of the titles given to the Virgin Mary. The Sun indicates the splendor of Glory which comes from God. The moon is the symbol of night and here indicates the powers of hell over which the Virgin Mary triumphs completely.

Great things concerning the New Reign of Jesus were revealed by the Virgin Mary at San Damiano in a lengthy message of immense import. This extraordinary message follows:

## Message of November 22, 1967

"The Father has given power to the daughter to fulfill her mission as Mother towards her children. He gives her power, He gives her help, He gives her strength and knowledge to accomplish all that the Mother of God asks for her sons because she wants to protect and save them with her very great love of Merciful Mother.

The Father, the Son and the Holy Spirit permit the Mother of all to walk on earth because she wants to save her sons, she loves them with so great a love.

The Eternal Father has given all power to His Spouse (the Most Blessed Virgin) to accomplish a great mission on this earth and to prepare all her sons with a pure heart, full of love, recognition and affection towards their Heavenly Mama, and to inflame all hearts for the coming of the Universal King upon this earth.

The Reign of Jesus will pour an ardent fraternal love into the hearts of her sons and will exterminate all the heresies, sin, all evil, and will throw all the demons back into the depths of the abyss.

68

All those who remain will have a great light and will accomplish something great, something very, very great on this earth!

Jesus will pass along the roads of the world with His Apostles, with the Saints and with the Angels, with all the Heavenly Court, with a perfume of Love, of great goodness and tenderness for all.

Jesus and Mary will always be with you, in the heavens, on the earth, on the ocean, together everywhere, in great joy and triumph with me.

And this bright star will enlighten the whole world with great joy for all those who will have suffered, endured, for my love.

Suffer! Suffer with me because your Mama of Heaven suffers so for her sons: especially for my sons of predilection (priests) who have forsaken me and my Son Jesus in great anguish. They were true apostles and now they have allowed themselves to be monopolized by diabolical temptation and they commit so many errors, so many sacrileges! But I still have mercy for them.

Unite yourselves, my sons! Unite yourselves, you who are here in my Presence. Pray, so that they may take hold of the arm of a loving Mother, Mother of the sons that I love so! That they may save themselves and also all the sons that Jesus has confided to them.

Reign of Jesus! Reign of Mary! In the entire world, in all hearts, with great joy and love! Confide in me, hope in me, and remain serene! Rest upon my Heart and do not allow yourself to be tempted, for the hour is approaching. The devil ferociously stands fast in the great terrible combat. He will not conquer because my Power will crush his head. Do not lose courage, my sons! Increase always in Faith!

But when this day comes when Heaven and earth will open, it will be a terrible battle of anguish and tears. Thunder and lightning will make a great din! But do not fear. Recite many Credos. Pray very much to Saint Michael the Archangel with the Rosary in your hands, that he give you strength, courage in the great battle. And you will be safe on earth and will win eternal happiness in Heaven.

When this calamity will be over and you see Heaven opened, it will be an immense joy for you, and you will never be able to comprehend the beauty, the grandeur, the goodness of the mercy of God !

Listen to me, my sons, listen to your Mama of Heaven who does everything for you! I left my Son Jesus in Heaven to come and save you, to give you a great grace and celestial blessing!

Prepare yourselves, my children! Prepare yourselves in this month with a heart gentle and serene, and do not be troubled for I am close to you, with your Guardian Angel, with Saint Michael the Archangel, with your Patron Saint. We will assist you minute by minute. Do not be troubled.

Pray! Pray! Pray! Always with a smile on your lips.

Those who must leave this earth will arrive in Heaven with a great company of Angels and will return on earth to comfort, to pray, to console all their brothers.

Listen to me, my children! Listen to me! It is I who am speaking to you! I am your Mama, the Queen of the Rosary, Miraculous Mama, Mama of Grace and Pardon. Put my words into practice and reflect!

Pray more, day after day, and you will have the strength to plod on with the cross on your shoulders up to Calvary where Jesus awaits you. There, you will find my Son Jesus, risen, at His Sepulcher. You, also, will rise to a new life of sanctity with the Angels and with the Saints.

I bless all those present and all those who will come to surround me and listen to my invitation. I bless you and I pour graces and blessings upon you."


The significance of such a message, its lessons, are absolutely incomparable. We will content ourselves here with listing some of the most important announcements:

- The extraordinary Mission of the Virgin Mary, sent by the Holy Trinity;
- The Reign of Love of Jesus;
- The defeat of Satan, driven back into the abyss;
- The unchaining of the elements;
- The extermination of heresies and sin;
- The great mission of "those who will remain;"
- The passage of Jesus on this earth with all the Heavenly Court;
- The constant Presence of Jesus and Mary, with everyone and everywhere;
- The tragedy of the consecrated;

- The terrible battle;
- The end of this calamity, the consolation of God, Heaven opened;
- How to prepare ourselves;
- The summit of Calvary with the Risen Jesus at His Sepulcher;
- Our resurrection with Jesus.

The above are only remarks. Such a message merits a very attentive and complete study. Have we observed, for example, the strength of the Madonna's words: "I have left my Son Jesus in Heaven to come .. ?"

Several points in this great message were confirmed in messages that followed. Jesus Himself would declare a short time later, during the period when the Liturgy has us meditate on the end of time and the coming of the Reign of Jesus:

"I Myself will come on this earth with many Angels, many Saints, many Patriarchs, many Prophets, and all the Apostles." (December 15, 1967)

26 janvier 1909 − 5 septembre 1981

Rosa Quattrini

## CHAPTER 5

## THE MEANING OF THE VIRGIN'S PRESENCE
## AT SAN DAMIANO

Why does the Virgin Mary come today at San Damiano? Each person can ask himself this question after considering the many aspects of these great Apparitions, as does one who withdraws after studying a reality in many different ways without fully comprehending it.

It is fitting, therefore, to pinpoint the significance and purpose of these Apparitions, in this place, in this day, in so important a manner. This is the purpose of this chapter.

**Giving Evidence of**
**Her Motherly Love**

"I have come down on this earth with you, to come and cry with you, to give you love. For a Mama does everything for her children. I want to give peace and serenity in your heart."
(December 16, 1968)

She is our Mother. We are her children. Her Presence is above all, an effusion of tenderness, that of a Mama who, coming to visit her children and before every other consideration, begins and continues by loving them, embracing them, and showering all her affection upon them.

This reality is poorly understood in our materialistic and utilitarian age. It is not understood that love is something gratuitous, inexpressible, irreplaceable, sufficient in itself and which has no equivalent: "Were one to offer all he owns to purchase love, he would be roundly mocked." (Canticle of Canticles, Ch. 8)

The Virgin Mary touches hearts in this display of tenderness (which we have already come to recognize by her words at the beginning of this book.) And a heart which allows itself to be touched is already converted. It is the Good Samaritan who, moved by compassion, does everything for his brother. It is Mary Magdalene who, touched by the recognition of Love, sheds her tears on the feet of Jesus and then follows Him up to the foot of the Cross. It is the Good

Thief, who, touched by the sight of Jesus on the Cross, takes His defense and asks Him for Paradise.

One must go to San Damiano with a childlike heart because the Virgin Mary comes herself with a Heart that is open, simple, with sincere attention, to embrace her children and give evidence of her Motherly Love with infinite delicacy.

Indeed, if there is one reality that humanity needs to be aware of, it is this! There is no greater love, none more deeply rooted in the human creature, than motherly love. But when this love rises and purifies itself to such a point, to that of the Virgin Mary, Mother of Jesus and Mother of all her children here below, it becomes an abyss, an ocean of tenderness and mercy, without stain or blemish, and at the same time, an abyss of humility, of compassion . . . "of everything," she has said.

The Maternal Love of the Virgin Mary, which God wanted for men and which was given to them at the foot of the Cross, is a foregone conclusion of mercy. Here, the words of Saint Paul are most applicable: "Charity . . . forgives all, believes all, hopes all, endures all." (Corinthians 1, Ch. 13) Maternal Love is blind. And God the Father has wanted to love us in Mary with this blindness of Maternal Love, i.e., with infinite mercy and compassion.

Humanity is in need of and thirsts for this love which is so great, so pure, so beautiful, so close. There are so many who no longer know that they are loved! This Love is like a ray of sunlight on our earth penetrating the prison of hardheartedness and strife which this world has become; it is a source of refreshment in the desert. There are so very, very many who have lost all trace of true love or who have never known it, who do not even suspect its existence!

And then, upon this dried-up earth, comes this smile so pure, this Motherly Love, these outstretched arms. Tears of Love, of Compassion fall, Sorrow for our sorrows; and roses and beautiful stars descend, rays of fire which penetrate hearts; and the beatings of this Sorrowful and Immaculate Heart, where each one is called to repose, to rest from the hardheartedness of the world, or even from the soul's own hardheartedness; already, mysteriously, even before the Great Light, hearts melt in contact with the Immaculate Heart of Mary and beat in rhythm with hers.

Songs rise and prayers mount from all hearts. The Virgin Mary, Mother of Jesus and our Mother, is surrounded by her children, fulfilling her Mission as Mother who loves them so very, very much, as she has always said. That is grace, a word which means: a gratuitous gift, a smile, favor, refound friendship, peace, serenity. These are the gifts that are poured into hearts.

Yes, in truth, the Virgin Mary comes to bring love anew on the earth and to imprint it with her tenderness. Blessed are those who "hear the Word of God and keep it!" "My children, I love you so much, so very, very much!" (April 8, 1966)

## To Save Souls for Eternity

"You must save your brothers and my sons at any cost. They must be saved, I repeat to you, my children!"
(August 20, 1965)

The Most Blessed Virgin Mary, our Mother comes in this world to save souls: to save souls for eternity. Jesus has asked, "What does it profit a man to gain the whole world if he loses his own soul?" And the Madonna has said repeatedly: "Everything passes here below, but eternity, never!" Heaven will last forever. Hell will, also.

We know that the Virgin Mary gave the children of Fatima a vision of hell to illustrate its reality. Rosa Quattrini was also given a vision of hell. This left her so terror-stricken that, for a whole month afterwards, she needed someone to be with her constantly.

The Virgin Mary recalls that she let her Son Jesus die on the Cross to save us. We must reflect, at the cost of our soul, upon the reality of eternity!

"I have come among you to save you." (December 22, 1967)

"I have come on this earth to save you." (December 29, 1967)

"I am on this earth to save you." (January 5, 1968)

"I am in your midst, my children, to save you, to give you all my love." (July 19, 1967)

Such declarations of the Virgin Mary are endless. She

has clearly specified and recalled that she comes to save souls for Heaven, for eternity. She then signifies the very relative value of material graces, of health or situation in life:

"Of what value are material graces if the soul becomes lost? The devil can also produce material graces but he has never produced any that are spiritual. I have come in this place to convert souls and to bring them, happy and serene, to eternity." (May 30, 1968)

"Of what value are material graces if after that, the soul becomes lost? My Son Jesus died on the Cross; but He died on the Cross to save you: to save your soul and to bring you one day into the Heavenly Fatherland." (April 5, 1968)

"My children, I am among you to bring you graces, consolations, and above all, conversions." (October 13, 1967)

The Virgin, our Mother, accomplishes this salvation through spiritual graces: conversions, repentance for sins, Faith, Hope, Charity, the family Rosary, reception of the Sacraments, Christian life according to the law of God and respect for life. There is concern for nothing else. There are not two laws, two Churches, two graces, nor two purposes.

She gives these graces abundantly in this place, chosen and consecrated for this extraordinary work of mercy by God the Father who has pity on the world. She gives them through her word, by evidence of her motherly love, in uniting all her children in prayer and sacrifice; finally, she gives them in the intimacy of hearts for, by virtue of her Mission as Mother of all her children, she has power to reach them, to touch them and convert them.

She does not cease to remind priests, parents, everyone, of their duty to do everything, suffer everything, accept everything to save their souls as she herself did at the foot of the Cross on Calvary where her Son was dying for the eternal salvation of all men.

Let us not imagine that these Apparitions, this coming of the Virgin Mary here below at San Damiano has any other purpose. The Virgin desires that we understand that the great work, the unique work is there, before which everything else fades away, and for which Jesus came, lived, suffered and gave His life: to save souls, to save souls, to save souls for Heaven, for eternity.

## To Save the Church of Peter

"I have come to save my sons of predilection. I have come to save the the Church of Peter." (January 19, 1968)

The Church is attacked, ridiculed and opposed on all sides. She knows her own deficiencies, her internal struggles, as we say; nevertheless, the attacks continue, left and right. Who, today, does not speak out against the Holy Father when he proclaims aloud the Faith and Christian morals? Who does not speak against the Supreme entreaties of the Church, against her hierarchy, against her priests?

The Virgin Mary has come to save the Church of Peter, i.e., the Church as Jesus founded it upon Peter as Head of the flock, Pastor of pastors; such as Jesus established and instituted it, with her Sacraments, her authority, her hierarchy, up to her Supreme Pastor here below, the Most Holy Father: rock upon rock. There is therefore no question of an intervention from Heaven which would lead to abolishing the structure of the Church, substituting a new state of things, without priests, without hierarchy, without Sacraments, without authority, without sanctity, without love. No, neither the Virgin Mary nor Jesus have ever said or wanted that.

The message of August 30, 1968 states: "The Eternal Father wants to destroy the Church of Peter. He wants to make it new (vuol farla nuova.) He wants Jesus to reign in love. He wants His sons of predilection to be poor in spirit, humble, charitable and pure."

These words have caused lively reaction and without a doubt, this is what the Madonna wanted: that we wake up! God threatens in order to save. God scolds in order to rescue and pull us away from evil. But if this text is read with discernment, we understand in which sense this renewal will take place (the Italian word "distrurgere" used here, and its Latin correspondent as well, have a more complete meaning than a "simple destruction"): poverty, humility, charity, purity - the words are there! This is what it is about! If we consider the text in its entirety and if we have reflected on the repeated declarations of the Virgin Mary, on her Will and her Mission to save the Church, we understand everything. And certainly, "to make new" the Church of Peter, is not to abolish it!

The Virgin Mary has said again and again:

"The Church of Peter must never perish. She must always triumph more in the entire world." (March 25, 1968)

"You will arrive at sanctity with a great triumph of the Church. For I am the Mother of the Church which will triumph in the entire world." (February 23, 1968)

"The Church of Peter will triumph always, forever and ever." (December 20, 1968)

The Triumph of the Most Blessed Virgin and the triumph of the Church are united, there cannot be one without the other. The Virgin Mary is the Mother of the Church and the Church is her daughter. The Mother recognizes her child and the child recognizes her Mother. This recognition, we understand, is extremely grave in face of the announced events.

The triumph of the Church supposes, on our part, respect for the Church. Men do not understand the protective care which God extends over what He has instituted. It is for this reason that men found it difficult to understand why the Virgin Mary, though her Heart was very sorrowful, guided Rosa Quattrini along the path of obedience to the Bishop's orders, particularly when this last one prohibited the transmission of the messages of salvation she was giving for all her children here below, especially for the young people and the Consecrated. The scope of such a drama is not understood. Nevertheless, as has been said, the Virgin Mary, come to save the Church of Peter, did not, and does not, want to act against the authority of the Church of Peter. This should be a source of much reflection for all!

We should not wonder that Mama Rosa, guided step by step by the Madonna, having received this promise since the first day of the Apparitions, kept herself in constant obedience to the Church and to the authority of the Church concerning the interdiction which forbade her to diffuse the Madonna's messages. She maintained a good Christian attitude towards her Pastor and the Masses that he celebrated according to the present liturgy of the Church. Everyone could know the state of her soul by observing her behavior. Rosa was a daughter of the Church; she never argued these questions.

At one time, Rosa was saddened to the point of weeping because particularly hard words had been spoken to a priest. She was grieved and protested with the greatest energy because 'a priest is a priest, he is consecrated, he is a representative of Christ on earth': "We must respect them, we must obey them, we must assist them!", she said.

There is no doubt that few places exist where there is so much prayer for priests, Bishops, the Church and the Holy Father as at San Damiano. The Mother of the Church and the Mama of all guided not only Rosa step by step, but guides all her children on the road of Faith and love. "In silence, all will be accomplished," are the Madonna's words.

**To Postpone the the Chastisements**

"With my Power, with the Sword of Saint Michael, with your prayers, we will lessen the chastisements."
(December 22, 1967)

The Triumph of Mary and the Reign of Jesus are events such that the human mind cannot even glimpse into except by the light of grace. They are events of triumph, a source of rejoicing and wonder for all the Angels in Heaven; they rejoice in the grace and mercy that God deploys in Mary which, in her alone, is a much greater work of Wisdom and Divine Mercy than all creation.

These events should arouse joy in all human hearts in an endless hymn to her who, so enriched with Divine grace, is also their Mother in the most real and loving sense.

In the light of the Virgin Mary's words at San Damiano and elsewhere, we can understand that in a new manifestation of His Mercy, God's design is to purify souls, all souls, for this great work of His Tenderness which will be the Triumph of Mary and the Reign of Jesus.

The chastisements are only a sequel, as the reverse side of a medal, rendered inevitable by the excess of evil. God does not think evil, does not want evil; His designs are Love. Chastisements are more repugnant to Him than to us.

"It depends on us not to have the chastisements," Rosa would later say in the Madonna's name. "We, by our prayer, by our cooperation, will have more abundant, more efficacious graces for soul and body, and the chastisements will pass." (August 20, 1965)

"Great chastisements will come. But is is up to you not to have them: it remains up to you." (August 20, 1965)

In His Mercy, God permits us to lessen the chastisements by our prayers and penance whereas His Own Son drained the chalice of His Passion in redemption for our sins.

However, the Triumph of Mary and the Reign of Jesus are a Triumph and Reign of Charity, Humility, Love, Innocence and Sweetness. The world cannot remain hard and impure. That is why the measure of the chastisements will be in accordance with our reparation, in accordance with the intercession, prayer and penance which should ward them off. It is this intercession, this prayer, this penance, that the Madonna asks of us at San Damiano, with her and around her. "Ask pity! Ask mercy!" These words have resounded in the messages countless times!

"Remain prepared! Remain in a state of penance! Because my Son Jesus, all wounded and scourged, is dying on the gibbet. You then, offer your sorrows and afflictions!" (April 5, 1968)

As Jesus said: "If they treat the green wood thus, how will it be in the case of the dry?"

The Virgin Mary invites us to remain prepared because the days can pounce upon us without warning: "I have told you to pray, to prepare yourselves through a good Confession and a good Communion; because if you are prepared, you will leave for Heaven and Jesus will be merciful to you. He will give you the kiss of pardon."

**To Prepare Souls for the Triumph of Mary and the Reign of Jesus**

"Let us prepare all hearts for my Coming and for that of my Son Jesus." (November 17, 1968)

John the Baptist prepared for the Coming of Jesus by preaching and by the baptism of penance. The preparation for the new Coming of Jesus must be the same. At San Damiano, the Virgin Mary comes to prepare our hearts for her Triumph and for the New Reign of Jesus on this earth.

She prepares us first of all because the events which

will inaugurate these great graces of Heaven will be fearsome. The Great Light which will be given not only in the sky but also spiritually in the depths of consciences, will transpierce souls and no one will be able to escape it: "It will rise from East to West and no one will be able to escape its ardor."

This Light will be much more dreadful for souls deep in sin and men would prefer every torment to this purification comparable to Purgatory, to this tearing of their innermost being, laid bare before the reality of Divine Love which they will have rejected. "They will be in the midst of a terrible struggle," the Madonna has said.

Blessed are the pure in heart who will see God! Blessed are the poor in spirit, the merciful, the peacemakers who already have the Kingdom of God in their heart and for whom the Light given by Heaven will be the same as that which burns in their heart!

But the Queen of Heaven prepares us above all for her Triumph and for the Reign of Jesus:

"I want your heart to be inflamed, burning with love for me. I will come with a great Light. But beforehand, your heart must burn with an ardent light for Jesus and for me. When I see you all reunited in faith and love, I will come with a great Light above the entire world and all will see me. All will listen to my word. Those who will have believed will have great joy in their heart." (August 22, 1967)

As we see it, the Madonna wants faith and love above all. In this respect, the preparation for her Coming and the New Reign of Jesus differ greatly from the baptism of John the Baptist which was one of penance only. The Madonna comes to prepare our hearts in love:

"My Son Jesus wants all your hearts to inflame them with love for Him. He wants to purify and sanctify them for His Coming." (November 17, 1967)

The Virgin Mary has come to set our hearts on fire with love:

"I have come to inflame your heart, to set it on fire." (April 5, 1968) **It is in the liveliness of intense love, a fire of love, that we must await the "Coming of the Universal King upon this earth."**

"The Eternal Father has given all power to His Spouse to accomplish a great mission on this earth and to prepare all her sons with a pure heart . . . to inflame all hearts for the Coming of the Universal King upon this earth." (November 22, 1967)

"I come to prepare your hearts in great love, in great charity, in great elan." (November 17, 1967)

"For this act of love you will have made, of offering your heart to the Divine Son, you will find much peace, much serenity, when He comes to triumph in the world through His Reign." (November 17, 1967)

# CHAPTER 6

## THE COUNSELS OF THE MADONNA

In all of her messages at San Damiano, the Virgin Mary does not cease indicating the Way to us. She does not cease giving her directives, her appeals, her invitations, her counsels, she whom the Church calls the Mother of Good Counsel and Throne of Wisdom. An entire book would be needed to make these appeals known in their immense diversity and astonishing richness. Here, in the limited framework of this book, we are giving only the main invitations regrouped around the principal themes.

**Jesus**
"Place yourself in the state of grace and remain in the state of grace."
(May 13, 1970)

Mary has given "Eternal Light to the world." Mary places Jesus in the arms of the aged Simeon. She again places Jesus on the altar of the Temple and on the altar of the Cross. Mary indicates Jesus, leads to Jesus, makes us contemplate Jesus, unites with Jesus.

The Virgin Mary's first directive at San Damiano is union with Jesus in the state of grace. This is the very essence of Christian life:

"Prepare yourselves constantly each day with Jesus in your heart. Even if must go to work, my children, receive Jesus one-half hour earlier." (September 8, 1967)

"Prepare yourselves with a good Confession and Communion and be prepared!" (February 21, 1968)

"Make a good examination of conscience and place yourself in the grace of God and you will be saved." (August 22, 1968)

To be in the grace of God or to have Jesus in one's heart is the very reality upon which the Madonna constantly insists: a reality conforming to the doctrine of Christian Faith and to the Love of the Heart of Jesus. With infinite sadness, the Virgin Mary brings to mind the fate of souls who die with mortal sin on their conscience:

"But for those poor souls who depart with a mortal sin

on their soul, a scorching fire approaches them when they present themselves at the Tribunal of God. It is the devil! And they are no longer able to talk. There are only howls between the soul and the devil who stands ready to snatch them and bring them into the depths of the abyss. This causes me much grief! I let my Son Jesus die to save you!" (May 24, 1968)

The Madonna has often spoken of the Particular Judgment when the soul appears before God, continually insisting, as did Jesus in the Gospel, on the necessity of returning to God while there is still time: "The Hearts of Jesus and your Mama are broken, seeing their sons lost." (April 8, 1966)

"I am here, my sons, in your presence, with my Son Jesus. Today is His Feast-day. His Heart throbs with love for men, to inflame them with such fire, so that you will love Him very much and approach Him with great love and much confidence. Jesus has His arms open and He has so much mercy! Implore! Implore peace, love and pardon, and He will give you everything.

Jesus is the King of kings: He can do everything and He can give you everything. Pray, my sons! Pray with faith! Consecrate all of yourselves to Him, soul and body, and He will give you such rewards and all the graces you desire. Love Him! Love Him! He was crucified for you! Why do you offend Him? Why are you so ungrateful? You do not want to recognize Him as King and He is the King of Heaven and earth! Reflect! Make a good examination of conscience! And you will understand all His Love, His sufferings, to save you." (June 21, 1968)

The Heart of Jesus and the Heart of Mary beat with the same elan, the same fire of love for us and in her love, the Madonna shows us the Heart of Jesus. (Rosa :)

"The Madonna says to knock at the door of the Heart of Jesus. Jesus is there, Who opens His Heart and lets me see His Heart opened, all love for us, and we must knock at His door . . . and He comes to comfort us, to console us." (June 25, 1965)

The abyss of Divine Mercy reunites with the abyss of human misery. Jesus waits. Jesus is all love, all mercy - to pardon, to purify, to inflame, if we come to Him: "The Heart of my Son Jesus is filled with burning love for souls and He wants to inflame all hearts. He desires that you understand His love that He gives. He waits, He waits, until all have drawn close to Him." (February 7, 1969)

We recall the words of Jesus in the Gospel: "You do not want to come to Me to have life!" (Saint John, Ch. 5)

"Jesus lives with love for you," says the Heavenly Mama, "and you, live with love for Him. Jesus is all mercy, Jesus is all love, all goodness and all kindness for His brothers." (August 19, 1968)

**The Sacraments and Eucharistic Life**

"Jesus calls you, Jesus waits for you at the Eucharistic Banquet to open His Heart with you, that you may give all of yourselves to Him." (November 29, 1968)

At San Damiano, we have seen the Virgin Mary's insistence upon the state of grace, also her insistence upon the examination of conscience, a good Confession and a good Communion.

The Virgin Mary also speaks very often of the baptism of little children because those who have not received it go into Limbo from where they will not leave to see the Light until the end of the world instead of today singing the Glory of God.

The Virgin Mary has also often spoken of the help priests should bring to the sick, to the dying. The Sacraments are the constant object of her exhortations, especially those which procure or restore the state of grace or those which nourish it, as the Eucharist. For above all, the Madonna's directives revolve around the Eucharist, there, where Jesus is. Alas, this attitude recalls that of Mary Magdalene more than ever: "They have taken away my Lord and I do not know where they have laid Him!" (Saint John, Ch. 20) The Virgin Mary essentially recalls the three principal aspects of Eucharistic life in her messages: Holy Mass; then during Holy Mass, Holy Communion; and finally, prayer and love towards Jesus-Host.

The Madonna asks daily assistance at Holy Mass with Holy Communion and that we not start our day without Jesus in our heart: "Go to hear Mass in the morning, receive Jesus in your heart!" (January 26, 1968)   "Go to Holy Mass! Because if you have heard Mass, if you have offered your day,  joined to prayer and sacrifice, in receiving Jesus in your heart, your Guardian Angel will smile at you when you present yourself at the Tribunal of God.  He will take you in his arms and bring you to the secure harbor." (February 2, 1968)

The Virgin Mary asks priests to celebrate Holy Mass with piety each day.  She asks the faithful to have Masses said, especially for the souls in Purgatory.

| **Love and Respect when Receiving Holy Communion** | "Jesus is real and alive, in the Most Holy Sacrament." (May 13, 1968) |
|---|---|

The Madonna insists upon the love and respect we should have when receiving Holy Communion.  She echoes the instructions again given by the Church in **"Memoriale Domini,"**  on the dignity with which we should receive so great a Sacrament:

"Changes brought about in such an important matter can also include dangers which will eventually be born by this new manner of administering Holy Communion (Communion in the hand), that is, less respect for the noble Sacrament of the Altar: a profanation of this Sacrament; an adulteration of the true doctrine.  That is why the Supreme Pontiff has judged that the traditional manner of distributing Holy Communion to the faithful should not be changed.   Also, the Holy See actively exhorts Bishops, priests and the faithful to zealously observe the law which has always been in force and which is hereby confirmed." (Instruction - **"Memoriale Domini"** - May 28, 1969)

Speaking in the same manner, the Madonna  recalls the solemn institutions of the Church in the ordination of priests:

"When they consecrate their sons, what care the Bishops take, what care the Holy Father, Paul VI, takes, to consecrate their hands! . . . The Holy Eucharist is trampled underfoot. My children take It in their hands!   My Son Jesus! Sacrileges upon sacrileges!"  (November 9, 1969)

The Virgin Mary instructs us as well on how to prepare our hearts for Eucharistic Jesus:

"My children, now I will explain what you should do to receive Jesus. Before going to the Communion Table to receive Jesus, prepare your heart. Call all the Angels and Saints and your Heavenly Mama in order that they accompany you to the Communion Table. You will receive Jesus with great happiness and love in your heart.

When you have received Jesus, do not leave right away. We must not leave without Jesus having entered into our heart, for this is an offense to Jesus. We must remain until Jesus is in our heart. Then, you receive graces, blessings and comfort. Only then can you leave the Communion Table.

Again call for the help of the Angels and Saints so they will come and thank Jesus with you for all the graces He gives you. Jesus is the King of kings. He can make you a gift of everything. He can give you everything. But you must receive Him with great love, great repentance for your sins and then Jesus will inflame your heart, He will set it on fire with love for Him and He will pour many graces, many blessings upon you and alleviate many of your sorrows." (November 8, 1967)

"Receive Jesus often in your heart, for you receive Him alive in the Eucharist and Jesus is merciful to those who receive Him !" (January 14, 1966)

"Pray for my consecrated . . . for they hold my Son Jesus in their hands ! His Body! His Blood !" (May 6, 1966).

The Heavenly Mama often speaks to us of the Tabernacle where Jesus remains night and day, adored by the Angels but abandoned by men to whom He nevertheless comes to give the infinite treasures of His love:

"The flame of love for Jesus in the Holy Sacrament must burn in your hearts. Jesus is the King of kings. He can give you so many graces! . . . Cast yourselves often at the feet of Jesus in the Blessed Sacrament. Knock at this little door where Jesus is always alone, weeping, calling souls into His Presence! Jesus opens all hearts to a great love, to a firm Faith, to an ardent charity, to a firm hope, to true repentance for all sins. Give all your sins to Jesus. He will destroy them and inflame your heart with love for Him." (February 2, 1968)

"Eucharistic Jesus is in the Tabernacle night and day

and calls souls into His Presence. He is alone with the Angels of Heaven, with the Archangels, who adore Him night and day. You, go also! Go, my sons! Go, and knock at the door of the Tabernacle where Jesus is alive and real, Who wants to talk to you, Who wants to give you graces, Who wants you to make reparation for the many outrages committed against Him. So many ungrateful Christians trample Him underfoot and make a laughingstock of Him, and profane Him in numberless places on earth! Jesus is always enclosed there, waiting for souls to make reparation. He waits for souls to console them, to give them abundant graces. Jesus is all Love. He is all Mercy. Jesus pardons those who ask pardon." (January 17, 1969)

"Make hours of Adoration before Jesus in the Blessed Sacrament." (May 17, 1968)

**The Christian Virtues**     "Love! Love! Love! That is what Jesus wants!" (April 8, 1966)

The call to practice the Christian virtues, especially Faith and Charity, is constantly repeated in the Madonna's messages. Insistence upon the virtue of Faith, associated with the recitation of the Credo, is one of the most remarkable directives of the Virgin at San Damiano: "I want Faith, Faith, my sons! Recite many Credos: it is through the Credo that I give you Faith. Ask for the graces you desire with great Faith. The Heavenly Mama will give you what you ask when you do so with great Faith." (October 13, 1967)

"When you feel weak, reinforce your Faith by a Credo. Repeat it forcefully. This Credo will reach up to Heaven with great joy and great love." (November 17, 1967)

The Madonna wants Charity. She speaks continually of the love Jesus has for us and of the love we must have for Jesus. She also brings to mind the love we must have for our brothers in our sentiments and actions: "Jesus calls you to Christian love, to fraternal love: love of goodness, gentleness, serenity.

I want love, my children! Love and pardon. Pardon! And when you present yourself at the Tribunal of God, Jesus will pardon you and you will enter into the eternal happiness of Paradise. My children, love one another and pardon one another!" (February 23, 1968)

"I want humility, not vainglory, not pride. Only love, love, fraternal love! Pardon, my sons, and you will be pardoned! Love, and you will be loved!" (February 16, 1968)

With the practice of the three theological virtues of Faith, Hope and Charity, the Virgin Mary asks for the Christian virtues, especially those of gentleness, purity, humility and serenity.

"Be humble, my children! Be always gentle and always serene!" (February 11, 1968) "Be humble, always gentle, always serene!" (June 2, 1968)

"Ask pardon! Humble yourselves! Be little! Not this arrogance, this pride, nor this malice! Trample on this pride! Be very humble and full of charity, very patient and persevering until death." (November 8, 1968)

## The Christian Family

We must also speak about the Heavenly Mama's insistence on the practice of family virtues and the duties of spouses and parents. Almost entire messages are consecrated to this. Some extracts are as follows:

"The union of marriage must be holy: in prayer, in love, in patience; everything is acquired through patience, with humility and charity: to pardon and to love!" (January 23, 1970)

"Take your heart, your love, to Jesus in the Holy Tabernacle and Jesus will enkindle such a fire of divine love, that discord will cease. There will be only peace. Think of the law concerning divorce! Promise me, my children, promise me, here at my feet, to love one another because your Mother weeps many tears of blood in beholding so many ungrateful children. They no longer want to love one another because of pride and arrogance." (January 27, 1967)

"You, also, mamas, it is up to you to educate your children while they are little. It is up to you to bring them to follow the way of sanctity, of humility, of purity. Keep them always close to you. Do not preoccupy yourselves so, mamas, with material things. You should think of your soul and those of your children.

Many mamas want to work in shops, in offices, and leave their children abandoned. For nothing but luxury! For nothing but the pleasures of the world! But they do not think they have a soul, their own, to save and those of their children! . . . It would be better to eat only one meal a day and remain united to your children, to your beloved, with love and sincerity . . .

Fathers and mothers, love one another and love your children! Fathers and mothers, pray and make them pray! Fathers and mothers, have no pride or malice; only love!" (December 27, 1968)

"Fathers and mothers, your children follow your example! According to the way you conduct yourselves, so also will your sons! . . . The Mother must set the example in the home . . . The mother must carry the cross with Jesus, in patience, in offering, in silence, and in prayer. . ." (May 6, 1970)

"Blessed be the families in which the sons are united to the elderly. I give much when they pray and love their children! My children, remember your parents and do not let them suffer! Keep them close to you; console them by your words, in everything. They have done so much for you! Why do you not understand them? When you also are old, and your sons make you cry and they do not love you, what will you do? Make a good examination of conscience and you will understand the evil and the good that you are doing.

Pray! Pray! Invoke Jesus who will give you many graces. You will have the strength and the consolation to give care, love, whatever is necessary. Do not tire of the elderly, but love them! Love them! Where there are the elderly, Jesus loves and consoles you more. Beside them, I diffuse numerous graces. Always be serene; serene always, in the happiness and peace of families. . . Pray always, be united always in harmony." (Feast of Saint Joachim, August 16, 1968)

The Madonna reminds the young people to love and respect their parents: "Imitate my Son Jesus: act as He did when He was on this earth! He showed love to all, especially to his parents.

You also, respect your parents! Love them! Obey them! Console them! Help them! Comfort them in all their necessities; they do so much for you!" (January 12, 1968)

Finally, among the other counsels that the Virgin gives, is her insistence upon silence. Certainly, we must speak of God, speak of the Presence of the Madonna at San Damiano, we must speak the words of charity, prayer. But the Madonna says we gossip too much; we must often be silent, following her example and that of the suffering, praying Jesus:

"Pray, make reparation, suffer, offer and be silent. In silence, you will find comfort; in silence, you will have graces; in silence, all will be accomplished and my Heart will triumph." (January 1, 1969)

"Pray in silence. Offer in silence. And I will do everything. I will accomplish everything according to the Will of the Heavenly Father Who sends me." (February 7, 1969)

**The Rosary**  "The Rosary, my children! I ask you for the Rosary in families. The Holy Rosary is the most powerful weapon to receive graces." (October 13, 1967)

The Virgin Mary has always insisted on the recitation of the Rosary in all her great Apparitions. We recall her requests at Lourdes when the Virgin herself recited the Rosary with Bernadette and where the Basilica was dedicated to Our Lady of the Rosary. The Heavenly Mama speaks of the Rosary at San Damiano and requests the Rosary in almost every message. Perhaps one could wonder at this insistence, considering the Rosary to be only a form of particular devotion. But this is a very thoughtless notion!

Is the recitation of the Our Father, taught by Christ, a particular devotion?

Is the Credo to be considered a devotion foreign to Christian life, when in reality it is a solemn summary?

Is not the Glory Be to the Father a recalling of the Holy Trinity, our God?

Is not a good part of the Ave Maria to be found in the Gospel, and was not the Virgin Mary in the center of the Mystery of the Incarnation and also closely associated with that of the Redemption?

Finally, is not the meditation on the Mysteries of the Rosary the summary of the whole Gospel and the reunion of all the Mysteries of our religion?

In truth, to find the Rosary strange would practically be the same as considering the whole Christian Faith strange.

The Rosary is a prayer that is well-balanced in its composition, it is gentle, harmonious and humane. Who has not experienced a cleansing of the heart and a re-finding of peace and serenity in the recitation of the Rosary? We obtain all graces through the recitation of the Rosary through the intercession of her whom God has truly made our Mother and through whom He wants to give us everything. But, let the Blessed Virgin speak:

"My children, it is the Crown of the Rosary that I announce to all my children. That they recite it often during the day! It is the most powerful weapon to receive graces and to save yourselves. The Rosary! The Rosary, my children! In families, in convents, in Churches!

The Rosary is the most beautiful prayer you can give me. Wear it around your neck. Carry it in your pocket. It is your defense against the enemy. It is your salvation. Promise, my children! Promise to recite it often! For in the Rosary is the prayer taught by Jesus, the Our Father. There is the Hail Mary. And there is the Glory Be to the Father, to the Son, and to the Holy Spirit.

The Father is He Who gives Power.

The Son is He Who shed His Blood to save you.

And the Holy Spirit is He Who gives you His Love and His Seven Gifts.

So, then, my children, promise! Promise to do everything to save yourselves with the Holy Rosary! Do this, and I will do everything to console you and bring you above!" (September 9, 1968)

The Virgin Mary especially insists that mothers recite the Rosary as a family and that they make their children recite it. How many mothers cry today because of their children! But, did they make them recite the Rosary?

"Mamas, pray! Pray for your children! Pray! Pray! For when you have left this earth and you see so many of your children in the abyss, how will it affect you?

For you no longer make your little innocent children say their morning prayers and the Rosary. Nothing! Nothing but television which is so harmful to humanity!" (March 29, 1968)

The Madonna, Mother of priests, also asks this beautiful prayer especially from them:

"My sons of predilection, take the Crown of the Rosary in your hands and re-assemble in great numbers the sons Jesus has given into your keeping. You will triumph in everything with the Holy Rosary and it will be the most powerful weapon in the moments of terrible trials." (May 8, 1968)

**Other Directives**

"My children, accept the cross with Jesus. Hold it tightly in your arms and imitate Jesus on the way to the road of Calvary."
(February 23, 1968)

It is impossible to make known in a few pages all the directives given to her children by the Madonna at San Damiano. We would have to speak of the ministry of priests close to the dying, of the education of children where the Madonna asks love, much love, but also firmness; we would have to speak of the souls in Purgatory, of the Particular Judgment, of hell, the devil and the terrible battle he is now waging against souls, and of many other things. Nevertheless, there are two subjects which must be mentioned: The Cross and the Angels.

The Virgin Mary followed Jesus on the Way of Calvary and accompanies us also on this road. She repeats the words of Jesus, inviting those who want to follow Him to carry the Cross with Him. The Virgin Mary reminds us that the Cross is beautiful when it is carried with love; that the Cross is the road of Heaven; that Jesus and Mary accompany us on this road; that the Cross saves souls.

**The Cross**

"My children, I am among you because my Son Jesus died on the Cross to save you and to give you peace and love. Always remain close to Him at the foot of the Cross, to carry the Cross with Him up to Calvary, with patience, with humility, with resignation and great love, in prayer. Such is the road to arrive in Heaven.

Accept the cross, my children: the one that Jesus sends you. Because without a cross, you do not arrive in Heaven. Offer it hour by hour in reparation for your sins, for those of your children and for the entire world. Persevere until death because you will be greatly rewarded above in Heaven." (May 3, 1968)    The Madonna invites us to carry the cross in silence because Jesus also was silent on the Way of Calvary.    She invites us to have recourse to the Sacraments, to the Eucharist and the Rosary in order to find the strength to carry the cross, and that we will find much strength and much comfort at the foot of the Tabernacle.

## The   Angels

"The Eternal Father is sounding the trumpet!  Give
the call!  Ring the bells!  The Angels are in the
world and they are ringing, calling all souls to me
so that they may be penitent  in  the love of God
and  with  everyone!
    Saint Michael will defend you with his sword!
    Saint Gabriel will console you!
    Saint Raphael will walk with you along the way!"

The Virgin Mary invites us to have constant recourse to the Angels for their help and assistance, particularly that of our Guardian Angels, but also that of Saint Michael, Saint Gabriel, Saint Raphael and all the Angels of Heaven.

There are two things we must understand:  First of all, the Angels are our friends, our brothers, and they want to help us.  Secondly, the Angels have power not only over things, but also over consciences.

If the devils have the power to tempt consciences by impressing and troubling them, all the more reason for the Angels to have the power to protect, enlighten and guide them; this assistance is willed by God in His plan of Love. The Angels can be a great and powerful help to us and it would be foolish not to have recourse to this powerful and necessary help.

"Pray very much to your Guardian Angel . . . Close to

me, he can do everything and he can give you many material and spiritual graces. Pray very much to him. Invoke him every minute of the day and night; that he defend you in temptations, in dangers to soul and body. Confide in him, for Jesus has placed a Consoling Angel at your side who will sustain and encourage you even in the most difficult trials if you have recourse to him." (May 24, 1968)

"As this day is dedicated to him, Saint Michael is having a great celebration in Heaven to glorify me, to love me, to sing many praises of love in the Name of Jesus and the Heavenly Mama, for he loves me very much!

Pray very much to him! Have recourse to him so that he can free you from the great evil the Enemy does to you. Insist! Insist through prayer. He is strong and with my help, can defend all of you for he is the Angel of Power, of Love, of Humility, and Gentleness.

Pray! Pray! Your prayer will be heard for he is prompt to wage battle. He gives strength to those who have recourse to him because Jesus gives him many graces to dispense and he is never inactive in Heaven. He comes to help (his brothers of the earth) in all necessities, all those who have recourse to him with simplicity and obedience. Pray very much to him, that he rescues you in life and in death. He can obtain everything from the Holy Trinity." (May 8, 1968)

### Message of Saint Michael the Archangel
#### July 13, 1967

"I have come here in your presence because, at my request, the Eternal Father has authorized the Heavenly Mama and the three Archangels to come.

**I have come to annihilate Satan, to make the Heavenly Mama triumph! I will lead you as long as you recite the Rosary.**

The weight of my presence will be upon your shoulders because the battles have already begun and you must fight with much strength. You must be strong, with your weapon of the Rosary, with my sword, and with the Heavenly Mama. .

**I am Saint Michael, your brother,** who assists you always, in all the moments of your existence and also at the hour of death, if you call me.

**Saint Gabriel** will announce all the things that are to

come. He will inspire and guide you.

**Archangel Saint Raphael** will be your companion the length of your journey that will bring you to the feet of the Heavenly Mama. She waits for you hour by hour, to give you consolation, comfort, peace and great love, the love of a Mother and Co-Redemptrix.

Do not torment yourselves, my brothers, if you are calumniated, insulted, ridiculed! Think of Jesus on the Way of Calvary. He was the King of kings and He was insulted, beaten and, always on the Way of Calvary, more insulted, beaten and calumniated than before! And you do not wish to endure anything for Jesus Who did everything to save you and Who died on the Cross for you!

Offer all your pains, your sorrows. Be humble always, my brothers, very, very humble. Act always with gentleness, serenity and with great love for your Heavenly Mama and her Son Jesus, Who love you very, very much and Who give you joy and consolation. You cannot comprehend the love we want for you!

The Heavenly Mama and Jesus send you a strong blessing which will assist you in life and at the moment of death.

In the Name of the Father, and of the Son, and of the Holy Spirit! Amen!"

Saint Michael also indicated the eternal value of prayer at San Damiano: "These hours that you pass here (at San Damiano at the feet of our Heavenly Mother) will be removed from your stay in Purgatory . . . **One minute passed here on earth equals more than a year in Purgatory!"** (12.22.67)

| | |
|---|---|
| **San Damiano** | "My children, run, run to feet! Come to supplicate me! Come to ask for graces!" (May 31, 1970) |

A certain number of the Virgin Mary's directives concern San Damiano :

The Virgin Mary calls all her children to her feet at San Damiano. Possibly certain ones would think that it suffices to pray from afar. Yet, the Heavenly Mama summons all her children around her in this place where she descends from Heaven to give them the comfort of her Presence and the inexhaustible graces that the Eternal Father gives her to pour upon her children in this place:

"Come to see me and love me, to thank me for the great gift I have given you, of coming on this earth to save you." (December 22, 1967)

"My children, come! Come! Do not delay! Come often to my feet, ask pity and mercy for all!" (January 19, 1968)

"Come often, my children! Come often when you are in tribulations and anxiety. Come here at my feet!" (January 26, 1968)

You will note the Madonna's purposes in summoning us: to thank her, to ask pity and mercy for everyone, to receive graces and individual assistance.

"Come! Come! Do not delay! Blessed are those who believe without having seen! Blessed are those who will have listened to my motherly call! I am all love, peace and mercy for you. Come! Come! Good-bye for the present! Good-bye!" (July 16, 1968)

The Virgin wants us to make her Presence known at San Damiano to save all her children: that we make her words known, that we make her graces known, for her Immaculate Heart must triumph in the hearts of all her sons in the entire world:

"Send my word to the ends of the earth, through your letters, in every manner. Write, speak, announce, that the Heavenly Mama comes to save you." (October 27, 1967)

"My children, speak! Speak! Proclaim that I am on this earth. All must know it, that I am on this earth to save you. Even if they do not want to understand it, tell them! Announce very clearly that I am the Mama of Heaven who comes to save you." (December 15, 1967)

## The Miraculous Water of San Damiano

The Miraculous Water of San Damiano which the Heavenly Mama says is the "most holy in the world," is of extraordinary importance because of its origin and because of the blessings it procures for men. It is given us through the Mercy of God the Father, the intervention, power and commands of Saint Michael the Archangel and the constant

97

intercession, presence and assistance of the Queen of Heaven and earth.

During the Apparition of Friday, October 21, 1966 the Eternal Father was present and said: "I give a special power to my garden here below, this little corner of Paradise, where I will dispense many graces." Rosa and those present saw a yellow globe cast down to the spot where the well was to be dug: in the garden by the pear tree. The Heavenly Mama then said that Miraculous Water would rise from this well, that it would be the source of spiritual and physical graces and that this Water would deliver the "possessed" if they had recourse to it with faith and believed in the power of the Blessed Virgin Mary. She then said: "Everyone will receive grace, strength, and some will even recover their physical health by using this Miraculous Water, because there will be no other water like it!"

Saint Michael was instructed by the Heavenly Mama to place his sword into the ground precisely where the well was to be dug, thus rendering it forever free from demons!

Rosa was given instructions by the Heavenly Mama regarding the depth of the well, that it must be covered with a little cupola and topped with a statue of the Virgin Mary.

In November, 1966, the Heavenly Mama said to drink from this Water of Grace: "Wash yourselves with this Water, purify yourselves with this Water, drink this Water and have confidence in it. Many will be cured of physical diseases. Many will become holy. Bring this Water to the sick and to the dying. Go often to visit the souls who are mourning. Be strong! Do not fear! I am with you! . . . This is the hour when the well will give light; it is a confirmation. Come, draw Water and take it into your homes and you will receive infinite graces."

Again, in December of the same year, the Heavenly Mama said: "My sons, drink this Water. It will purify you in soul and body . . . drink it often! Come to this fountain which will make many souls more holy, giving light and faith to their hearts."

On the Feast of Saint Philip Neri, May 26, 1967, Saint Michael gave a message of great import regarding the protection the Miraculous Water will give us during evil times and further explained how we are to prepare and draw this Water from the well:

"I announce that all must prepare large plastic containers in order to take much Water . . . and prepare little basins.

When the great moment of disaster arrives, because they have not listened to "Her" word, many gases will be sent into the world, many evil things, plunge your face in this Water which has been poured into basins and you will be safe. . . .

When the family comes to draw Water, before filling the container, they must pray ten Ave Marias and say: "Miraculous Madonna of the Roses, save us, and deliver us, soul and body!" Through this prayer, much Water will spring up, and with this Water, we can reunite ourselves and be saved.

Prepare all of this very quickly.

Prepare little basins for the Water in which to plunge the face.

Pray with faith to the Heavenly Mama and the Eternal Father to have the strength and courage to endure all.

When you feel these great shocks and see the great darkness, lift up your eyes to Heaven and with open hands, ask pity and mercy through the recitation of three Salve Reginas and five Credos. Cry out with all your heart: "Jesus, Mary, save us !" For these will be hours of anguish and tears especially for those who will not have believed in me ! . . .

Oh, my sons ! This Water brings light, love, peace, health, into your homes. May it be your strength, your power against the diabolical powers that will come to overwhelm you and the whole world.

In the Name of the Father, the Son, and of the Holy Spirit! Amen!"

The Heavenly Mama said that Water from this well will always be plentiful, enough for the whole world:

"Much, much Water will spring up from this well, enough Water for the whole world, to refresh all, soul and body, to console them, to give them peace, love, serenity on this earth and great peace and joy above in Heaven." (July 16, 1967)

Before drinking the Miraculous Water, one prays three Ave Marias and the ejaculation, "Miraculous Madonna of the Roses, deliver us from all evil of soul and body."

If one applies the Miraculous Water to an ailing part of the body, one first prays the Credo, then the three Ave

Marias and the above ejaculation to the Miraculous Madonna.

## The Blessed Handkerchiefs

The Most Blessed Virgin gave us another precious gift on November 11, 1968:

"Bring many little white handkerchiefs. Put them in a small nylon bag (simple precaution in case of rain) and place them all in my little Garden. You will give these handkerchiefs to many sick people and they will wipe away their tears.

This handkerchief will receive a great gift from me. Those who wipe their eyes with it will have the light of Heaven : they will understand that Jesus calls them: they will understand that they must prepare themselves in penance and ask pardon, to arrive in Heaven happy and content.

This is a great gift I give you, my children; a great gift the Eternal Father has given me to save my sons! Tell this to everyone! That all can run here, that all come to love me, that all can come to receive graces for this life and be brought above." (November 11, 1968)

The Heavenly Mama would soon repeat:

"My children, the handkerchiefs! This is a great gift I have given you, so great ! So great !" (December 19, 1968)

Rosa has also specified: "The handkerchiefs must be kept on one's person. If one is in trouble, if there are difficult trials, if one is in tears and confusion, then one covers one's face with the handkerchief and makes a Sign of the Cross. Also in the moment of cyclones, calamities, one passes it over one's face to have the light of Faith. For the conversion of sinners : when they place the handkerchief on them, on their eyes, they will have the light of Faith, whether they be sick or not."

Rosa says these handkerchiefs can be small through necessity or convenience. After they have been blessed by the Heavenly Mama ( at noon on the First Friday of the month ) , they can be washed, but never bleached, cut or ironed.

Concerning the subject of the Blessed Handkerchiefs, we must recall what is related in the Acts of the Apostles on similar graces accorded to the first faithful:

"And God worked more than the usual miracles by the

hand of Paul; so that even handkerchiefs and aprons were carried from his body to the sick and the diseases left them and the evil spirits went out." (Acts, Ch. 19)

In a more general manner, the use and the grace of these handkerchiefs are registered in the Christian tradition of the use of sacramentals : holy water, blessed candles, scapulars, etc., but we must not forget that the grace accorded them is immense.

## The Chaplet of Faith

"I announce that you must recite the little Chaplet of Faith . . . At the beginning, you recite the Credo and then you say ten times: "Jesus, Mary, I love you! Save souls! Save the consecrated!" Instead of the Pater, you say the Credo. At the end, after having thus prayed the five decades, add five Salve Reginas to obtain peace between brothers of the entire world. All reunite yourselves with great Faith and great love for Jesus! Do not fail to recite this little Chaplet of Faith every day: one day, you will be so happy, so content!' (July 7, 1967)

The Heavenly Mama continually stresses the importance of the virtue of Faith : "for a strong Faith is necessary to overcome all the obstacles that will present themselves." And Jesus tells us: "The Faith is the most precious gift I have given you. Do not waste it . . .!" (November 22, 1968)

Among the Old Testament figures exemplifying the virtue of Faith, we can consider Noah as an example for our most distressing times. His simple strong Faith never wavered during the one hundred years it took to build the ark : "Now faith is the substance of things to be hoped for, the evidence of things that are not seen."

. . "By faith, Noah, having been warned concerning things not seen as yet, prepared with pious fear an ark in which to save his household . . . he was made heir of the justice which is through faith." (Hebrews, Ch. 11, v.1, 7)

We recall that the ark is also symbolic of Mary, who has been given the title of Ark of the Covenant. And at San Damiano, the Heavenly Mama tells us: "Come under my mantle while the Angels, Archangels and Saints hold it wide open to cover all my children of the world. Do not wait until

101

the Eternal Father closes my mantle again because then there will no longer be time to lift up your eyes to Heaven to ask pity and mercy." (April 14, 1968)

## A Great Sanctuary

The Madonna has asked that a great Sanctuary and Church be built at San Damiano - a Church with fifteen altars, one for each Mystery of the Holy Rosary.

# CHAPTER 7

## PARTICULAR MESSAGES

The messages given by the Virgin Mary and Jesus at San Damiano are habitually addressed to everyone. However, in certain cases, the Virgin Mary or Jesus speaks to a specific person or to a specific category of persons by reason of the importance of their mission. This can be verified, for example, in what concerns parents in the preceding chapters.

The principal persons concerned in such messages are the Holy Father, Paul VI, the consecrated and the young people. In this chapter, we will make known the messages, or excerpts therefrom, which relate to them.

Certain messages about Rosa Quattrini will be found here as well in order to better clarify her vocation and the reality of San Damiano.

Few comments will be made and the greatest care will be taken to present these important texts as an ensemble of documents before each conscience.

### The Holy Father, Pope Paul VI

> "The Holy Father is a holy,
> holy soul on this earth and I
> will give him every help and
> comfort. He is my favorite,
> I love him so . . . for he loves
> you so!"        (May 6, 1967)

### An Account of the Apparition of
### September 1, 1967

Rosa: "The Holy Father is arriving with Saint Michael and Saint Raphael. The Heavenly Mama presents a red cope and a white one. Jesus blesses them, takes the red cope and places it on the Holy Father's shoulders. There ia an Angel holding three roses and he places them in the hands of Jesus.

"Jesus gives them to the Holy Father with a palm in his right hand. Jesus kisses the Holy Father on the forehead."

(Rosa weeps.)

"My brother, be strong! Strong! Strong! Speak clearly to the world that all may understand you and that all may love Me! I, Who am the Son of God."

Rosa adds: "Jesus places the white mantle on him. Jesus and the Holy Father kneel down, their hands raised towards Heaven, looking at the Eternal Father."

These words were pronounced by Rosa with much serenity, many gestures and profound emotion.

### Extract from the Message of February 2, 1968

"The Holy Father suffers so! We should unite to him in prayer, in sacrifice and in love, to help him carry his cross which is so heavy. He is the Head of the Church and the Church must triumph in all and for all."

### Extract from the Message of December 20, 1968

"Pray! Pray! Pray! For the hours are sad. Especially for my son, Paul VI, who is in the midst of a terrible struggle filled with anguish and tears. Pray very much for him. Make a sacrifice so that he can have the strength and courage to embark in the world to give Faith and to speak clearly to all. May the Holy Spirit enlighten his mind and inflame his heart to burn only with love for Jesus. Jesus is always with him. Jesus lives with him night and day in suffering and tears.

Why do you not listen to him? Why do you not listen to his counsels? He who listens to him, listens to me. He who follows him, follows me. He who threatens him, threatens me."

### Extract from the Message of February 2, 1969

"You should give much happiness to my son, Paul VI. Console him! Love him! Be close to him through prayer, through sacrifice, in all ways, because he is your Father. The Holy Spirit will enlighten him with a great light to give light to all his sons of the world."

## Extract from the **Message of February 7, 1969**

"Pray for my consecrated son, Paul VI, who is the Father of all the fathers of the world, who carries the Cross with Jesus, with serenity and love, to save all the sons Jesus has confided to him. His sufferings will change into such joy!

Follow him! Imitate him in his humility, in his patience, in his love, in his silence!

Open your eyes! Open your heart, my children! Listen to him! Listen to him! For the Holy Spirit is always upon him and I who am his Mama of Heaven, hold him under my mantle and follow him step by step on the road to sanctity and drive away all those who want to harm him.

Pray very, very much for him! For he himself prays for you day and night close to me. Jesus and Mary are always close to him: we walk with him and we suffer with him at the sight of so many ungrateful sons, so many conceited and proud sons! The devil is fighting with strength but these are his last hours. For my power will crush his head and he will no longer be able to ravage."

## Messages to Priests

"It is the terrible hour, we are in the terrible hour! It is the hour for priests to re-awaken the hearts of men! Priests, open your arms! Open them wide! Press your stray sheep close to you, embrace them, bring them into the sheepfold, for the hour is terrible." (August 6, 1965)

> "I love my sons of predilection so much! I love them so very, very much! I want to give them my love, my joy, my most tender caress. I want them all saved."

## Extract from the **Message of October 6, 1967**

"My sons of predilection whom I love so very, very much, do everything to console my Heart which suffers so. Console me! Make me known! Make me loved!

I am the Queen of Heaven, the Mother of the Universe. I

want all my sons of predilection to become saints for if they themselves become saints, all my sons that Jesus has confided to them will follow the way of goodness.

My sons of predilection, I want all of you under my mantle. I want all of you saints, great saints, as when Jesus walked the earth. He showed His love to all, consoled all, assisted all, especially the sick. You also, approach the sick, my sons of predilection! Console them! Give them resignation, peace of heart. Prepare them for the road of Heaven. For, how many souls go to perdition because there is no one to encourage them, no one to give them a token of love.

But through your prayer, through your Guardian Angel, you can do everything. I will give you strength, power and all the heavenly graces to conquer every obstacle that will arise. Offer everything to my Heart: sorrows, calumnies, persecutions. I will give you graces, comfort, joy.

Be strong, my sons! Do not allow yourselves to be conquered by temptations! I want you always little, little, like Jesus in the crib. I am a Mama of Love, of Mercy and Pardon. Only one look of repentance, and I give you the kiss of pardon on your brow."

### Message of May 8, 1968

"My sons of predilection, take the crown of the Holy Rosary in your hands and gather together in great number the sons that Jesus has given you to watch over. You will triumph in everything with the Holy Rosary and it will be the most powerful weapon in the moments of terrible trials.

Carry Jesus in the streets and make hours of Adoration before the Blessed Sacrament. Have recourse to Jesus so that the Eternal Father has pity and mercy and that He enlightens all souls in order that they accomplish their Christian duty.

Penance! I ask penance of you, my sons of predilection! Ask for help and mercy for all and for all the sons that Jesus has confided to you. If you promise, you will receive.

Your Mama promises you and gives you all that you ask and gives you strength and courage to carry the cross with Jesus, for your mission is grave, especially in these confusing times. But you must be strong, humble and

106

patient, with great purity of heart and be persevering until death. Jesus wants you holy apostles and holy martyrs like the first Apostles who gave their lives for Him.

Saints! I want you saints, my sons of predilection, I who am the Queen of Apostles and Mother of the Church, who wants to save you, who wants the Reign of Jesus to triumph in the entire world, in all hearts, and that my sons of predilection be the consolation of the sons Jesus has confided to them.

My sons of predilection, be always little like Jesus in the crib. Endure everything. Summon everyone close to Jesus in the Blessed Sacrament. Unburden yourselves to Him. Jesus will open hearts, purify hearts, inflame hearts with love for Him and will pardon everyone, for He is so merciful!

Promise me! Promise me, my sons of predilection, me, your Mama, who calls you to prayer and penance! Listen to my call of a Mother who weeps so to see my sons so ungrateful. A Mama does everything for her sons! I am the Co-Redemptrix, the Mother of Mankind, the Mother of the entire world, who let my Son Jesus die and who assisted Him up to the last hour to save you. Listen to my moans as my Heart is transpierced by a sword of sorrow, anguish and tears.

Open, open your hearts, your mind, your mouth! Ask pity and mercy while there is still time! Open your hearts with Jesus while you celebrate Holy Mass and ask the Eternal Father to purify and sanctify you and all the souls Jesus has confided to you.

Lift up your eyes often to Heaven and call me by the sweet name of Mother and I will open your eyes to the light of Jesus Who is your Brother, true Apostle and Salvation for all."

## Message of Jesus to Priests
### December 6, 1968

Extract -

"I am the King of kings. I love you very much and I want My apostles to be all around Me like a great host of Angels; I want all My apostles to be holy, that all be pure, very humble and always poor in spirit, that all may follow Me on the road of Calvary, close to Me, because if they are holy, they will then save souls, they will bring many souls into glory and to salvation.

My apostles, may your love be only for Me and for My Mother, who is also your Mother. May your heart be inflamed with love only for Me! Your heart should burn with love for Me. Your body will be trampled upon, but your soul, white as snow.

Embrace the cross, My apostles, very, very tightly in your arms, your hands! Endure everything for My love because on this earth, everything passes, but eternity, never! In this eternity, the Eternal Father awaits you and there, your Mama of Heaven welcomes you in her arms of a very loving Mother. Do this, My brother priests : with Christ, in Christ, and through Christ. You must live and die as Jesus has called you to do. Your life must be only a sacrifice, your life must burn only with love, your words must be only comfort, encouragement and resignation for souls."

## Message of Jesus to Priests
## August 4, 1969

"My beloved brothers, I ardently desire that all My priests would remain around Me, love Me with the same love I have for you, with the same mercy that I extend to you.

I want you to be little, always humble, for your mission as apostles is so great on earth and in Heaven! Your life should be one of holiness, humility, purity, charity towards all the sons I have entrusted to you. *You must guard, sanctify and love them, not with your own love which is earthly, but with My love, for it is I whom you represent in this world!*

You must remain lost in contemplation with Me, then you will understand everything, but you must be poor ; being poor, you will understand your Brother in the countryside of Bethlehem. Neither riches nor honors are required, only love and charity for your neighbor, for if you walk in the way of holiness, all are able to follow you and love you.

Be little, be little, My brothers, without arrogance,

pride or malice. Your presence in the world should resemble Mine ; always smiling, even though it be difficult, and bear the cross as I bore it. Thus . . . slanders, betrayals, injustices and later, they still had to nail Me to the Cross . . You also must follow Me; take no heed of the world. Think rather of this : If you have performed your mission, that is, to become holy, when you die the gates of Heaven will open and you will enter, escorted by Me, by My Mother, by the Patriarch Saint Joseph and by the entire Heavenly Court.

Certainly, were you to think of what places are yours in Heaven, you would no longer concern yourselves with worldly affairs, but only with the salvation of souls! There lies your way to Calvary, with Jesus, through Jesus, and in Jesus!

*Bear in mind that you are My brothers, for your hands are consecrated and so is all your being ; that upon your person, you may carry Jesus, Alive and Real, so as to give Jesus to souls. Only you, no-one else ! It is you who represent Me here on earth ! Remember this . . . do consider this!*

Do not think of worldly ambitions and the pleasures of this world, think only of the One whom you represent here on earth. If you think of the latter, all men will love you, all will praise you, all will come to you and seek words of comfort, a word to assist them in bearing the cross without complaint. There are so many souls who die in anguish for lack of resignation, because they receive no comfort from My brothers . . . How I suffer because of this ! Think . . . think . . . and meditate!

*When you are celebrating Holy Mass and taking within your hands, My Body, My Blood, My Whole Being, during that moment of the Consecration , you may ask for any graces. If it is for the good of your soul, for all souls, you may receive whatsoever you ask.* Ask, ask, ask for peace in the world, for love in the world, for repentance and a saintly life, as the first Apostles lived.

Speak, speak to mankind. Approach souls, comfort them, for the world is filled with deceit. Men no longer have compassion for one another, no longer do they love and forgive one another . . . but when the time comes for departure from this world and they present themselves to have their sentences pronounced, will it be the same ? . . .

Only the Truth remains : Either Paradise or hell. So many of My brothers are lost and some are imprisoned in Purgatory where they suffer the most agonizing penalties because they have not fulfilled their mission as Fathers.

You are the Fathers of the earth ; you must love every soul indiscriminately, the good as well as the wicked, and you must bear everything in order to sanctify yourselves.

Ask the Eternal Father for the light, for the strength required. Ask the Holy Spirit for His love, His Seven Gifts. May the Holy Trinity give you much strength in all things !

*Make My Mother and yours loved and known for she comes on earth to call you, to bring you the Holy Rosary, to save you . . .* The Eternal Father has given her much power. She can do all! She calls, she loves, she does all to save her children on earth. She calls you under her mantle and guides you on the way of perseverance, day after day . . . for everything will be fulfilled !

*Love her ! Love her and make her loved ! This is your duty, My beloved brothers, to make her loved, since she is the Mother of the Church and the Queen of Apostles. She can give you all !*

She is calling out and inviting you into her embrace to free you from error and temptations, for the Enemy is very furious and is devouring many, many of My brothers, many of Our apostles - My Mother's apostles and Mine ! What sorrow My Mother feels as she sees so many of you being lost, so many of you who have the Church as your Spouse !

*You think of the earth . . . and the devil divests you of your reason and you no longer understand My love nor the love of your Mother, the Mother of the Church.*

Pray . . . all pray, those whose minds are still clear, for through your prayers and sacrifices, you can bring your brothers onto the way of sanctity . . .

My beloved brothers, be strong . . . because the hours of sadness are drawing near. What will become of you if you heed neither Me nor Our Mother who keeps calling you night and day to save you, to pardon you and give you the kiss of love ?

Ponder at the foot of the Cross. Make an examination of conscience and you will find enough strength to dismiss all worldly ideas and embrace Jesus, your Brother ; follow Him up to Heaven, for I await you.

I am with you. I am above you. Walk, walk on My way and you will receive eternal happiness. I want all of you to be inflamed with My love, that you may be purified and loved. "

## The Young People

"How I weep to see so many of the young going to perdition ! I would like to see them all filled with happiness, all with love in their hearts, and all with Jesus. And I would clasp them to my Heart."

(May 5, 1968)

Extract from the **Message of April 8, 1966**
**To Children**

"You other little children, go to receive Jesus ! Lead your papa, your brothers, close to Jesus : that all may receive Jesus in triumph, in peace ! That He may bring peace in all hearts and in the entire world.

Pray, little children ! Pray, because Jesus listens to you. He gives you all the graces you request. "

## Message of Jesus to Children
## April 5, 1969

"My little children, all innocent and beautiful, who give Me all love, I am Jesus, here in your midst.

How happy I was in your midst! What consolation you have given Me, My little children, all reunited around Me!

Always be happy! Always united in prayer! For it is in prayer that you will find the strength, the support, the encouragement, along the way you must travel. Walk always on the way of sanctity. Walk always in joy.

Love your parents and all those who follow you, who approach you. Be only love for everyone, for when I was on this earth, I called all the children around Me ; I gave them much love. And you, give Me much love also ; even if I am above in Heaven, I see you, I hear you, I follow you step by step. For I want all of you reunited to Me one day in Holy Paradise."

## Extract from the **Message of August 5, 1967**

"Pray for everyone, pray, my sons! Pray especially for the young people who are so in mire and who make me weep very, very much over the sin of impurity, who do not listen to my motherly word. I moan so, and weep tears of blood. My Heart is broken.

Implore, my sons! Speak to the young people! Speak with gentleness, with love. Send your Guardian Angel, that he make them understand that they do the Will of God. Without Me, without my Son, one can do nothing.

Pray united! Pray very much to the Holy Spirit in order that He enlightens the young people, that He places them in the Peace and Grace of God - for the hour has struck, the hour has struck! The Eternal Father no longer temporizes. Pray among yourselves, with me, with all the Holy Angels of Paradise. Insist, insist, my sons, with prayer and sacrifice. He will have pity and will be merciful."

## Message of Jesus to the Young People
### Easter, March 29, 1970

"Young people, how I love you and how I thank you, you who have listened to My Mama and yours in the call to come here at the Heavenly Mama's feet!

When I was on this earth, I so loved the young people! And I want to love them so! I want to fill them with joy and love, strength in the Faith, in order that they come to rejoin Me one day above in Heaven.

Do not think so much of here below! The greatest beauty you will see above, among flowers and songs, love and joy, with the Angels and Saints.

You will see the Splendor of the Eternal Father. You will see the Splendor of the Holy Spirit who has given you all His love. You will see My Heavenly Mama and yours who will cover you with kisses.

I will give you a great light. I will put so much love in your heart! Revive the Faith, My sons! Revive the Faith! I am here among you to fill you with graces, to fill you with love. For I want to live alone with you in your heart. I want to destroy all sins. Give Me all your sins : I will destroy them and will inflame your heart with love for Me. Live only in love for Me! And die only of love for Me, to rejoin Me above!

It is so beautiful above, My children : to meet everyone again! All your dear ones are there : parents, brothers, friends, everyone! They are there in the midst of a field of flowers, among the lilies and perfumed roses. *

I also want the perfume of your love. I also want all your love because I want to give you all My love. And with My love in you, you can give it all to your companions, to your sisters, to your brothers, who are far away : that all may awaken in love. For My Mama, and yours, is calling you, calling you day and night under her mantle to embrace you and fill you with graces.

Your Guardian Angels have inspired you and you have listened to the call of My Mama and yours. I am so happy to see so many of My sons around Me and My Mama! My Heart experiences such joy !

I am risen! You also must rise with Me, to live only with love for Me, for everything passes on this earth, but eternity, never! Never!

You can always be joyful in the world but do not sin, My children, do not sin! Sin is grave. It leads to damnation! However, I died for you ; but to bring you to Heaven, to glorify you in Heaven ; to sanctify you on this earth and then to arrive in triumph above, with the Angels and Saints.

The Angels pray very much for you, especially your Guardian Angels! All the Saints in Heaven, the Holy Souls in Purgatory, they all pray for you : that you become saints, that you may enter into Glory without entering Purgatory. For when you see My Splendor, it will be great! . . . Great! . . . Great!

Listen to Me! Listen to Me! And listen to My Mama and yours, who calls you to penance, who calls you to love, who calls you to prayer, to purify you, to sanctify you, to rejoin the Heavenly Fatherland.

Be happy! Be happy! Joyful with Me! *For when joy is the Joy of Jesus, it is everything !*

My children, I want to inflame your heart with much

---

* We recall the words found in Canticle of Canticles : "My Beloved and His flock who feeds among the lilies." (Canticles, 2: 16)

love! I want to set your heart on fire with a great joy. Be strong in the Faith, I repeat it : Be strong! Because Faith will help you to overcome all the obstacles which will arise . . . Live for Me! Die for Me! To rejoin Me in Glory!"

Extract from the **Message of Friday, May 1, 1970**

"I will place My great love in the hearts of men, in the hearts of the young. The young people should be as a rose blooming on earth. The young people! . . . hearts blooming . . in my Heart . . . in the Heart of Jesus . . . the Ardent Lamp to all!

Young people, wake up! Young people, sin no more! The sin against purity brings eternal damnation. Think, and think again that everything passes very quickly but eternity will never end. When you will be above in Heaven in my arms, how you will sing with the Angels and Saints, what joy you will experience!

"Young people, I call you, I call you to my feet! Listen to me while there is still time for you! I repeat this so many times. I love you so! When Jesus was on this earth, He also called the young people around Him. He surrounded them with love, tenderness, mercy. You also, have recourse to Jesus, my Son, who will have mercy and pardon you. Promise to no longer offend Him, to revel in Him one day in Heaven!"

**Rosa**                "I have come in this world to make use of this 'instrument' that she may speak clearly to the world." (Nov. 23, 1966)

### Message of December 1, 1967

During the recitation of the Rosary, Rosa announces the Presence of the Heavenly Mama with Jesus and at the Fifth Glorious Mystery, she says:

"Jesus, I am not worthy that You come close to me but only say one word and I will listen to You! I am a miserable sinner! I am a poor ignorant one! I am nothing!"

Now, Rosa repeats the words of **Jesus:**

"Because you are nothing, I want to cover you with My mantle. I want to come close to you to inflame your heart with love for Me."

Rosa then says that Jesus descends to the earth. Rosa kneels at His feet, asking pity and mercy for all : "Save us, Jesus!"

"Yes, My daughter : I will inflame your heart with such love, such gentleness, that you can give it to all. Pray! Suffer! And be silent! All for the salvation of the world, in order that they may recognize that the Heavenly Mama is here in this Enclosure. **This will become the International Center of My Heavenly Mama.**

My Heavenly Mama chose you for Her instrument because you are the most ignorant. But you must love her very, very much, with a very great love. Suffer! Suffer, My daughter! That all may believe that it is the Heavenly Mama who comes.

They come here with malice, with pride, with pretence. But the Heavenly Mama scrutinizes their mind and heart. She knows everything : how they come."

Standing up, Rosa again implores pity for everyone and now repeats the words of the **Heavenly Mama :**

"My children, I am here with my Son Jesus whose Heart is broken by such great, great sorrow! By so great an offense! Pray, all of you, reunited! Come here with great Faith, with great love, for Jesus wants to give you so much love. He wants to fill you with love, heavenly joy . . . "

### Message of March 1, 1968

This message is reproduced in its entirety with the account of scenes and dialogues which constitute the first part. Jesus and the Virgin Mary speak in this message.

**Jesus:** "My little one, you must not fear. When I was in the Garden of Olives, I also was abandoned by all. I had only the Eternal Father to assist Me. You have not only Me beside you; there is the Heavenly Mama who covers you with her mantle. You must not fear : Forward! Forward, My daughter! We are there, close to you, giving you strength and courage to stand fast. Forward always with Jesus and Mary. Jesus is with you. The Heavenly Mama covers you with her mantle. You must not fear! Forward, My daughter! I tell you, forward! Rest upon My Heart and I will inflame your heart with love for Me."

115

Rosa, very touched, overwhelmed: "Jesus, I am not worthy to be close to You! Have pity on me! I am a miserable sinner! Help us! Pardon us! Comfort us!"

**Jesus:** "Courage, My daughter! Courage, My little one! Courage! Embrace the cross with Me, I will give you all My Passion. Follow Me!"

Rosa: "I am ready, Jesus. I will accept all that You desire. I offer You my life, all my being, and also all my sins. Destroy them! Inflame my heart with love for You! That I can come from this earth to revel in You, above in Heaven!"

**The Heavenly Mama:** "Do not fear, my children, I am among you. My 'instrument' has said many times : give me all the crosses you want! I have given these crosses. This confirms what I have said, my children : her crosses will become heavy but she will accept everything."

Rosa: "Yes Heavenly Mama, everything! I accept everything for Your love. It is enough that You cover me with your mantle and hold me to your breast. I am even ready to accept death : everything for your love."

After a long pause : "Yes, Jesus, I am ready to accept everything. Give me all the crosses. I am ready to accept everything. Welcome me with You, Jesus. Have pity on me and the whole world! I offer You all my sins and all those of the world. I am ready to suffer, Jesus, all that You want. Give me everything! It is enough for me that all the souls, all, will enter into Holy Paradise with me. But I want all to come there. Make me suffer everything for Your love. But all the souls must enter into the Glory of Holy Paradise."

**The Heavenly Mama:** "Yes, my daughter, I promise you, you will suffer in a hidden way. You will suffer with great love for me, with me, close to me. I will give you everything : strength and courage to suffer with me. Always embrace the cross. Always have the Crucifix in your hands and press it to your heart. My beloved daughter, as my Son Jesus told you : you are my 'instrument,' . . . very little . . . but with much love."

Rosa again renews her offering and prays for the whole world, especially for the young people.

**The Heavenly Mama:** "Pray, my children, because the Sorrowful Passion of Jesus has already begun. I am beside Him, Who suffers and moans. You, also, follow me.

Offer your sorrows, your afflictions, hour by hour. Offer some sacrifices, some good works : many little flowers are possible, my children. Do it for the love of Jesus.

*Observe some days of fasting, at least on Thursdays and Fridays.* Do it in order that our hearts may be all reunited together, to ask pity and mercy of the Eternal Father for my sons.

Keep yourselves close to me, my children, very close to me under my mantle while it is still open to pour out so many graces, so much mercy! I will give you very many blessings which will descend upon you from Heaven, my children!

Courage! Forward!

Christus vincit! Christus regnat! Christus imperat!

*Be strong in the battle which is about to break loose! Then I will come with a great Light to awaken all hearts, to convert souls and bring many to Heaven.*

Jesus calls you! Jesus awaits you! Meditate on the Passion very often during the day. Make the Way of the Cross and meditate on it. Promise love and fidelity.

I am your Mama of Heaven who watches over you, above you, and pours graces, a rain of roses along your way. Ask for graces!

**Do not fear, my children! Do not fear for my Triumph! I will come! I will come!** But I want souls to be converted, that souls may understand that it is I who comes, my children! For I am the Mama : Mama of Sorrow, Mama of Mercy, Mama of Pardon.

My children, listen to my motherly word. Listen to it and put it into practice. For I have suffered so very, very much! I suffered so on my way of Calvary. More than you! Suffer with me in silence, in prayer, in sacrifice.

Accept, accept, my children! One day, you will be so rewarded! When, one day, you will be in the Glory of Holy Paradise! You will be filled with joy, triumph, songs, love, grace. You will see my Son Jesus and your Mama who burns with love for you.

Yes, my children, I will pour many, many graces along your way. But remain united in prayer, in sacrifice and in Holy Communion, for Jesus is the King of kings above you. He will do everything. He will give you everything. And He will console you.

In the Name of the Father, and of the Son, and of the Holy Spirit!   Amen."

# CHAPTER 8

## THE CITY OF ROSES

**The City of Roses is the dawn of the New Reign of Jesus.**

The "City of Roses" ... these words echo in the ears and hearts of many, enveloped with a heavenly perfume and also with mystery. They justly recall the other known words, "The Garden of Paradise." They are as of the same source. They bring to mind the gifts of Heaven, of the "Miraculous Madonna of the Roses." After hearing well-qualified explanations, it is well understood that these roses will not only be of the earth; they are concerned not only with a "Promised Land," an announcement of happiness, but also with graces, a renewal of hearts. "City of Roses," words chosen by the Madonna and we well know what she means when she speaks of the Garden of Paradise, of the City. We understand the Heavenly Mother, her heart-spoken words.

But the mystery remains and a thousand questions could be asked: "What will be the scope, the true reality of this City?" ...

"And then, why so distant?" The remoteness adds to the mystery. Why leave the pear tree, the blessed Garden? ... Finally and above all, if the works have been announced, they have not yet been completed. Will there truly be a City there, the heart of which will beat for the entire universe? A "City of Roses," that is, a work whose structures will extend with order and where we will flourish only as roses of divine grace and love that Jesus has just cast upon this earth? Roses of charity of the Hearts of Jesus and Mary, inflaming all souls, for a world resembling her Garden of Paradise, a world of purity, love, humility, but in a new dimension, in the perspective of the Triumph of Mary and the New Reign of Jesus? ...

Yes, this City will come to be ! The Madonna asks, and has been asking for a long time, for homes for orphans, for the aged, the sick, the destitute, calling to mind the many, many abandoned young in the streets and marketplaces who no longer have anyone to care for them and love them, to save their body and soul. During a particular apparition, Rosa announced:

"Beside the Holy Father are seven little children of each race, from all parts of the world, who represent the Seven Spiritual and Corporal Works of Mercy." Rosa invited the Franciscan priest who was present to list the Works of Mercy:

## The Seven Corporal Works of Mercy

1. Feed the hungry
2. Give drink to the thirsty
3. Clothe the naked
4. Visit the imprisoned
5. Shelter the homeless
6. Visit the sick
7. Bury the dead

## The Seven Spiritual Works of Mercy

1. Admonish the sinner
2. Instruct the ignorant
3. Counsel the doubtful
4. Comfort the sorrowful
5. Bear wrongs patiently
6. Forgive all injuries
7. Pray for the living and the dead

Rosa then continued with the Madonna's words:

**The Madonna:** "I have already announced so many times that I want many homes, to feed the children who are dying in the streets and marketplaces; many of the aged, many mamas who are suffering, moaning!"

Horrified, Rosa sees them. She then resumes the Madonna's words spoken to the priest present:

**The Madonna :** "Speak to people, my son, in order that all may understand that I want many homes in which to shelter these little ones ! They are brothers like you ! They are mothers like you ! They are fathers like you ! They are sons like you ! You should take care of your brothers !" (January 5, 1968)

Since the earliest times at San Damiano, the Virgin Mary has declared that she wanted a great Sanctuary in this place as well as numerous homes to welcome the poor, the orphans, the young people, the handicapped of every kind who would come and who would be in need of shelter :

"I want a great Sanctuary and many, many homes in which to shelter the many homeless children." (December 8, 1966)

"I want all my sons to unite as brothers, in love, in peace, in harmony, and prepare many, many homes here, close to me, there where I have come to bring joy . . . do everything possible to make my Sanctuary." (December 9, 1966)

"I want a great Sanctuary: it will be the reunion of peace, of harmony between all, and the salvation of the whole world." (January 6, 1967)

"A day will come when you will have such light! When you will have such consolation, such joy! . . . In this Sanctuary that I have announced to you and which you will make and these homes for the Consecrated which you will prepare . . . for the abandoned children, for the poor, for all . . . Begin these works! Do not wait too long! Reunite yourselves! Reunite yourselves in prayer and works so that when the chastisements arrive, the young will all be reunited under my mantle." (March 10, 1967)

But we will understand nothing of the City of Roses if we think only of its material construction! What good is it to construct a body without a soul ?

No, the City of Roses is not only a work of temporal beneficence to be added to the many others on this earth for in so doing, one could not contest its merits nor its efficacy.

To better understand, one must ascend as does one who climbs a mountain in order to discover what has never been seen before; without so doing, one cannot have a proper idea. In order to obtain a proper comprehension of the City of Roses, one must ascend in the understanding of the great prophetic announcements of San Damiano and in the intimate knowledge of the Hearts of Jesus and Mary. We must make this effort of ascending in order to see. Great prophetic announcements are made by the Most Holy Virgin in her messages at San Damiano. They reunite perfectly with biblical prophecies and with those already formulated by the Virgin in preceding apparitions, particularly at La Salette and Fatima.

These announcements concern the Triumph of Mary in the whole world and the New Reign of Jesus : two events which are linked and which are nearest. The following words of the Gospel could be repeated word for word : "This generation will not pass away until all this has been accomplished." And the Blessed Virgin at Fatima announced: "Toward the middle of the second half of the twentieth century."

Of what will the Triumph of Mary and the Reign of Jesus consist ? It will be the destruction of all the evil and all the works of evil on the earth and the coming of the Reign of the Hearts of Jesus and Mary. It is through the power of Mary that the Devil, author of evil, will be driven back into Hell, according to the prophecies contained in both the beginning and the end of the Bible (Genesis and Apocalypse.) "It is only through her intercession, to whom God has given the power to crush the head of Satan, that we will have the decisive victory." (Message of Saint Michael, May 26, 1967)

"I will come with a great light and I will triumph in the entire world; my Son Jesus will come with a New Reign and will bring peace and love, tranquility and joy into hearts." (May 13, 1967)

**"And this brilliant star will enlighten the whole world with great joy for all those who will have suffered, endured, for my love ! ...** Reign of Jesus ! Reign of Mary ! In the entire world, in all hearts, with great joy and love !" (November 22, 1967)

"These candles (represent) Jesus who will come in His New Reign. He will bring peace, love and victory in all and for all." (June 2, 1967)

We think of the City of Roses when we again read these words : "I come to prepare your hearts by great love, by great charity, by great elan ... !" (November 17, 1967)

"I will come in a great light, but **beforehand, it is necessary that your heart burn as an ardent light for Jesus and for me."** (August 22, 1967)

" ... Beforehand, it is necessary ... " : **we understand that the City of Roses will be at one and the same time the hearth where this fire of love originates and sustains itself while awaiting the coming of the New Reign of Jesus, and the Place of predilection which will manifest itself on the great day of Mary's Triumph in the entire world.**

**It is already of Place of grace where Heaven tends this seed of new life which should spread out over the entire earth : a seed which begins in**

works, in hearts, in souls, and even in things - the Reign of Love of Jesus.

When pilgrims began to flock to San Damiano from different countries, efforts were undertaken to respond to the Madonna's repeated requests for the material realization of the City. Nevertheless, as is habitual in great works willed by Heaven, all kinds of difficulties delayed their realization : material difficulties, administrative difficulties, unforeseen obstacles sprang up at the last moment.

Yet, little by little, by means of the very modest gift offerings of the multitude of pilgrims and in spite of the high bidding, some land was acquired and several buildings have been renovated, especially around the Place of Apparitions. This work was of primary importance, made necessary at this time by the anxiety to guarantee the respect of this place and by the need of welcoming at least a minimum of pilgrims - their tents and other means of travel.

But the Madonna insisted! She wants a great international work which must not only be a place of welcome for a few pilgrims. Here, we must pause in order to properly understand this immense realization that the Madonna wants, in humane and spiritual dimensions that are completely new and extraordinary. The Virgin Mary indicated what this immense work must be in her message of March 25, 1968 :

"I want an International Center of the entire world (Un Centro Internazionale di tutto il mondo) : a City of Roses; a Sanctuary, the greatest in the world."

In the light of the Madonna's numerous declarations on the international character of San Damiano, on the grace which is given there, on the necessity of welcoming and saving the young people, we can understand that this work which the Madonna calls City, and City of Roses, must be of immense proportions involving three great purposes of charity, especially toward the young.

The first purpose is a material welcome. The Madonna's work at San Damiano daily assumes international dimensions on a worldwide scale for the salvation of all, especially for the young, as the Eternal Father willed by sending the Virgin Mary here below to save all her children.

The Virgin Mary is there. Nothing can prevent her from being there. Nothing can prevent her from touching the hearts of the entire world. Thus, the pilgrimages assume considerable dimensions and the Heavenly Mama watches, she who is a Mother, to welcome her children. We must respond to this necessity. All these pilgrims must be welcomed in a decent, humane and Christian manner.

The second purpose is the achievement of a more stable organization for a more lasting welcome, for the young above all, because of their readjustment and reeducation so that, moved by grace, they will pass from the world of drugs, despair and moral decay to reimplantation into a Christian world.

This supposes, first of all, an organization with structures and people who would offer a material, humane and moral welcome. This is what the Madonna wants. She wants us to help in the building of this great work. She does her work herself through the grace which converts souls, through her maternal love. She wants us also to do our part, in works through fraternal love. The Madonna has told us : "You should concern yourselves with your brothers!" It is not easy. But, if the Madonna is truly present at San Damiano, with her help we can bring our own, if we so will, if we have Faith and if we love our brothers.

This work of arranging and planning is now in progress, due to the acquisition of vast acreage.

But it also supposes the existence of those Christians who must welcome the young. In fact, the young people themselves will build it, each helping the other. The class struggle must be substituted by the union of hearts, as Jesus said : "That they be one as We are one." Then, and it is the Madonna's Will, must be realized in the City of Roses, a world truly according to the Heart of Jesus, Christian in all its structures, methods, mentality, principles; a world opposed to the chaos presently reigning on earth; a world which will be the beginning of the New Reign of Jesus.

Indeed, the Madonna wanted the City of Roses to accomplish her works. She wants homes for abandoned children, for the perverted, for drug addicts. She wants the work to be as a perfumed rose for her sons who are returning to purity. This rose signifies the innocence of the Love of Jesus, the Purity of Mary, humility, charity. That is why she wants the City of Roses : to form the Reign of Jesus, of Love, in souls.

She does not want her sons thinking of so many worldly things. She wants the salvation of the soul because it is the salvation of the soul that matters, on earth and in Heaven. If the soul is saved, all is saved : "What does it profit a man to gain the whole world if he loses his own soul?" This is evangelical realism. This is what the Madonna wants. For, in Heaven, it is the eternal felicity of the Love of Jesus. The Madonna has come in this place, sent by the Eternal Father, because not since the beginning of the world have there been such terrible moments as now : in the Church, in the entire world. Therefore, the Eternal Father has sent her to save her sons. As she saved the world in the time when she let Jesus die for the salvation of her sons of the earth, she likewise now comes again to save her sons of the earth because so many souls are going to hell! Because no longer is there purity. No longer is there love. No longer is there humility. No longer is there charity.

The third purpose of the City of Roses is then, an encounter between Heaven and earth, in the perspective of the Madonna's great prophetic announcements at San Damiano.

A rain of roses pours from Heaven upon San Damiano : a rain of graces, abundant graces, which touches souls, converts hearts, restores lost souls to sanctity and returns to the Heart of Jesus those who have been led astray. This place of graces must grow. The Blessed Garden must become a City of Roses; for the City of Roses will be the radiant extension of grace of the Garden of Paradise. These graces will cause many flowers of purity and charity to blossom! The Heart of the Madonna must beat in all hearts. Her Place, Her City, Her Garden of Predilection will be there, where a welcome will be found, a rebirth, the bearing of much fruit, so many souls regenerated by grace. It will be the new dimension of the Garden of Paradise, new in the dimension of the new arrival of pilgrims, the young people of the entire world. "They must be saved!" the Heavenly Mama, their Mother, has said. It will be the implantation of the first seeds of the New Reign of Jesus, where Jesus will reign in the midst of souls that will truly love Him, souls that He will have set on fire with His Love and that will remain in

His Love.

At the same time, it will be the fruit of our earth : fruit of our constructive efforts of the love of the Madonna and fraternal charity. This is the part that depends on our poor human hands but which Heaven awaits. It will be the fruit of sanctity, purity, fervor of the young, humility of heart as Jesus wants on this earth. There, songs will rise which will no longer be concerned with war, or revolt, or discord; instead, there will rise anew towards God the perfume of prayer of pure hearts, the same prayer as that of Jesus. There, through human hearts which He has saved and which the Heavenly Mama has saved, Jesus wants to make rise anew to His Father His prayer of thanksgiving and love as He prayed it on Holy Thursday evening.

**The City of Roses is the dawn of the New Reign of Jesus.**

According to the words of Jesus, love is poured upon the earth from the bosom of the Most Holy Trinity : "That the love with which you have loved Me be in them, and I in them" (Saint John, Ch. 17), as it is presently poured out at the Blessed Garden from the hands and Heart of the Most Blessed Virgin. "Love comes from God," reiterates Saint John (John, Ch. 4). The Most Holy Trinity is the Hearth and Source from where love is precipitated into humanity. It is this love full of tenderness and strength which must set fire anew to the world and which Jesus wants to cast again upon the earth. It is this love which will convert hearts, which will touch them in the most intimate manner, to make the City of Roses a Kingdom of purity and peace, where very many will be converted and saved, the penitents on fire with a recognizing love. The Eternal Father wants to purify and renew the world in love. It is the very tenderness of the Eternal Father, the Holy Spirit and the Word made Flesh which will penetrate souls. The Holy Spirit will be diffused as a Fire which no one will be able to resist. The Love and Power of He Who Is will be felt in every heart. But this charity will also be poured from the transpierced Side of Jesus and from the Heart of Mary, associated in our salvation.

The Virgin Mary will be highly glorified in this work. Her work of Love, her Mission of Love, will be her Triumph at the same time. The two will be one. "I will do everything for you. I will come with a great Light and I will come on this earth with the Reign of Jesus, Reign of Love and Mercy . . . A great Light, resplendent with sanctity, will come and it will reawaken your hearts." (November 21, 1967) "Pray, my children, for I will come with a great Light and I will triumph over the whole world and my Son Jesus will come with a New Reign." (May 13, 1967)

The Triumph of the Most Blessed Virgin will be the Triumph of her Immaculate and Merciful Heart. It is this extraordinary grace which is already the source of conversions at San Damiano, the like of which we have never known. It is this same richness of grace which pleased God to deposit in the hands of Mary, which will cause flowers of purity and charity to blossom in the City of Roses. Nothing can stop this grace and her Triumph will be total for the salvation of all the hearts which will be opened to her motherly love, in humility and charity. "Blessed are those who will understand a Mother's love!" (April 5, 1968)

That is why the City of Roses will be a Garden of Graces, Innocence, and Love for all the little, the humble, and the rejected, the abandoned and the outcasts of this earth. It will be the New Garden and the Ancient Garden at the same time, in the words of Saint John, where the world will be reborn such as Jesus created it and always wanted it to be, and remakes it with new vigor after Satan has had the power to reign for a time on earth before being driven back into the abyss beneath the feet of the Most Blessed Virgin Mary.

The rebirth of creation will be more beautiful than its first birth; humanity will be more afire with love. It will be the Garden of Holiness for all those who will work in the service of the Madonna and their brothers, living in prayer and sacrifice in the example of the most fervent religious and as they already do in the Place of Apparitions. It will be the Garden of Mercy for all those who arrive there, whatever the weight of their sins, throwing themselves in the arms of a loving Mother. For, the Heart of the Madonna wants to rekindle, purify, renew and save many souls of her children, all souls : all those who come and also those who do not come and whom she awaits and calls with all her motherly love.

We understand then that the City of Roses will be a New World. It will be the restoration of creation in its first dignity and of Christian life in charity, humility and purity, the reverse of the reign of Satan. The methods, the hearts, the minds, and even things, the principles of culture, art, education, medicine for the body and soul, reeducation of the perverted, drug addicts - all will be restored and reestablished according to the Reign of Jesus and the laws He instituted since creation in the world of men and in minds, thus making His Power , His Wisdom and His Merciful Love burst forth more than ever, especially upon those whom the society of Satan has ruined.

The Light will also rise on them. They must see that they are loved, those that no one wanted ; that they find Faith, those that the world knows only to throw upon the waves of uncertainty, doubt and despair, in this hour when Pastors declare they are in search of them.

We recall the magnificent words of Holy Scripture which the Church has us sing at the approach of "Blessed Hope" : "Behold the Lord will come, and all His Saints with Him. And on that day there will be a great Light. Alleluia!"

"O Orient, Splendor of the Eternal Light and Sun of Justice! Come and enlighten those who are sitting in the darkness and shadow of death!"

And again, these words of Scripture : "The needy and the poor seek for waters, and there are none; their tongue hath been dry with thirst. I, Yahweh, will hear them. I, the God of Israel, will not abandon them." (Isaiah, Ch. 41)

"The people that walked in darkness have seen a great Light and to them that dwelt in the region of the shadow of death, light is risen." (Isaiah, Ch. 9)

"O King of Nations and object of their desires! The Cornerstone which reunites the two peoples in You! Come and save man whom You formed of clay!" (Antiphon, Time of Advent)

# CONCLUSION

Several thoughts are proposed for the reader's consideration at the conclusion of this brief summary of the facts of San Damiano :

Is is true?

Is it an accurate truth that the Virgin Mary comes on earth today in such an extraordinary manner?

In answer to this question which many could ask, as though incredulous before a reality which does not seem possible, we offer the following for reflection :

First of all, God is Father. He does not abandon His creatures. In the midst of the greatest distress the world has ever known, God sends the most merciful, most loving help. For this, God has chosen the Virgin Mary in the immensity of her maternal love and in the profusion of graces He has given her to pour upon her children in this place. Let us reflect in our consciences if that conforms to the Power, the Wisdom and the Mercy of God.

Following, it must be noted that the Virgin Mary's words which have been scrupulously transmitted into this book - the author so affirms, before God - are words of love, accessible to all. It is a language of complete love. May we reflect well, here again, for it is the most certain sign of the works of God. May we ponder upon other known and recognized Apparitions, may we ponder upon the Gospel and on what Saint Paul calls "the language of the Cross," which scandalized the pagans as well as the Pharisees.

We want to draw attention to the very simple yet very original style of these messages. Because they are simple, a superficial reading could leave a superficial impression. These are things of God and not of this world. The prophecies given at San Damiano are presented nowhere else in such profusion or intensity. It does not seem reasonable to attribute such an ensemble to pure human invention. The source would not be as pure, as shining with Love and Truth, nor would it be new, humble and discreet before the world.

Great conversions have always had Truth and Love as their source. These are the two signs by which we recognize God. Often our mind is too worldly and prevents us from discerning them, as the Pharisees said of Jesus : "Can anything good come out of Nazareth?"

Let us draw near then, with a pure heart, in humility and charity. It is "when silence enveloped all things, and night had already reached the middle of its course," that the "All-Powerful Word came from the Royal Throne of Heaven." (Liturgy, Sunday within the Octave of the Nativity)

With a pure, humble and poor heart, let us consider if this word is truly marked with the Sign of God made Man : "Full of grace and truth."

And if we have recognized it, let us follow it!

# ROSA QUATTRINI   1909 - 1981

Rosa was entering her seventy-third year when she was called to Heaven on September 5, 1981, the First Saturday of the month. Her Funeral Mass and burial was on September 8, 1981, the Feast of the Nativity of the Blessed Virgin Mary. In remembrance of this humble little rose of Northern Italy, we recall some of the heavenly words spoken to her :

**JESUS:**   "I bless your prayers and multiply them so that there will be a new sunrise that will bring about the renewal of the Faith with blessings for the faithful and for the world."   (November 22, 1968)

**THE MOST BLESSED VIRGIN MARY:**   "Remain in peace close to Jesus and your gentle Mama of Heaven. One day they will understand you, my daughter - when you  will be with me above in Heaven."  (May 13, 1968)

And the Heavenly Mama's words to Rosa of the victory of San Damiano:

"The day will come when the bells of San Damiano will ring in celebration, to give me glory and honor, and for the Reign of Jesus!" (March 25, 1968)

## TESTIMONY OF FR. LUDOVICO BONINI
### Chaplain to the state hospital of Fidenza (Parma), witness to Mama Rosa's last hours

"When Mama Rosa first arrived at the hospital at Fidenza, I was curious to see her for she was known only by hearsay.

I found myself in the presence of an elderly person, sweet and simple, of whom I grew fond. Her stays in the hospital became frequent and prolonged. She was 'home' there. Each time she came to the hospital, one was aware of loving her more. Little by little, she entered into one's heart like a family figure. There was in her something fleeting, something which escaped one just when she was about to reveal it and one could only think of the mystery she carried within herself.

Then I understood the charm and the fear of this mystery - her suffering. Her life and her mission were reduced to, and concentrated on, suffering.

Suffering makes one humble and transfigures the silence. Mama Rosa accomplished this continuing task in her life - to reduce everything to the essential. Silence and prayer were the atmosphere she created about her. By silence, she was present to herself; by prayer, she was present to God. And thus she fulfilled the sacrificial aspect of her suffering.

The illness which struck her progressed and spread throughout her body. Then there was the suffering of her spirit, that will to be near the crucified Lord, the fear of not knowing how to remain there. For this reason, she always called upon the will of God and day by day completed her sacrifice in offering her cross to the Lord. Now she had truly become the Madonna's disciple.

She passed the time with rosary in hand, learning anew the difficult lesson of acceptance and experiencing the joy of giving. One had the impression of a confident familiarity between the Madonna and Mama Rosa.

The pain and the problems, always inexplicable to us, found in the spiritual climate of that soul a surprising clarification : a new understanding (easy to be said but not to experience) that through suffering one could offer oneself in self oblation.

The greatest desire that Mama Rosa expressed was to receive the Holy Eucharist. The essential requirement of her spiritual life and of her mission in the Church was to become a holocaust, or rather to accept the desire of being offered, burned, consumed like a flower, like a candle, like a victim, symbols quite present in her life history.

Through suffering and great faith in the Eucharist, she had acquired a vision clear and great of her work - the sick whom she thought about more than herself. She had Masses celebrated for them and recited the rosary.

During the Christmas of 1980, she gave me holy cards to give to all the sick in the hospital and candy for the sick children.

An aspect of her devotion which struck me was her familiarity with the angels and in particular, Saint Michael, to whom she made novenas. From the simple and restrained way with which she spoke of the angels, I seemed to grasp that she lived as if on the threshold of the invisible where man reaches out of himself not to dream or to escape, but to live his true reality.

Her conversation, soft but never verbose, gave one an intuition of aspects and realities which one does not think about even though they are obvious by faith.

Mama Rosa was again admitted to the hospital in the first days of September, 1981. Although accustomed to see her suffer and endure, this time she seemed overcome with pain. But her only expression of it was labored breathing.

On the evening of September 4, she received the Sacrament of the Sick. It was the consecration of the victim in a suffering body. The sacrament seemed to have brought a little calm but later in the night, she deteriorated greatly.

Summoned by the faithful Emilia, I hurried to her bedside to recite the prayers for the dying. In her drowsiness, the sick woman, as if holding her breath, followed the prayers which implored the divine mercy to free this soul and take her to Jesus in Paradise. 'May the Virgin Mary, the angels and saints come to meet you.'

It seemed destined that Mama Rosa's earthly existence would end thus. She had already received the Eucharist in the preceding days, when in extreme prostration she asked to have Jesus brought to her (that is how she would ask for communion.) While I hesitated, fearing she would be unable to receive, she assured me that she was able to do so.

I went to the chapel and brought her the Eucharist. She gathered all her strength, composed herself serenely and then invoked Jesus. She said the ritual prayer and received the Viaticum.

It was like the encounter of persons who were always awaited, with the trepidation and emotion of a definitive meeting.

She also made her thanksgiving as usual, with lucidity, but as if in haste while still able to complete it. Absorbed in prayer, she dominated her suffering.

Meanwhile, we were not able to repress our emotion. The children were nearby as always with their affection and tenderness. Emilia was there. The staff on night duty were there. We were there to contemplate, not death, but a passing. In fact, it was not the approach of death that was visible in Mama Rosa but it was her absorption in Jesus. She seemed to be no longer of this earth.

The simplicity and silence which surrounded her illness now surrounded her death. Her breathing grew weaker, almost imperceptible, until it ceased. The sorrow and agitation of a death was not in us, but the serene peace of an arrival. All of us perceived that we were spectators of something unusual.

"Jesus !" , the name pronounced, which gave life to the rite of the Sacrament and to death, was the light which pierced the darkness.

Was it a cry in the night ?

Was it the prayer of supplication in pain ?

Was it a vision of departure ?

Certainly a drama was enacted, but in the peace of the Lord. Death with its mute language perhaps unveiled the secret which an entire life carried with it - the cross for a mission of good, but also for others to follow."

## ROME - WEDNESDAY MAY 13, 1981
## ASSASSINATION ATTEMPT ON THE LIFE
## OF POPE JOHN PAUL II.

### J.M.J. Pilgrimage Group Present On This Fateful Day

We thanked the Madonna of San Damiano for a safe arrival in Rome and looked forward with great anticipation to the general audience of the Holy Father.

As is the custom, one must obtain a pass at the Vatican Office on the day preceding the general audience at which time the area of seating is assigned; but our late arrival required that we visit the Vatican Office on the very morning of the general audience. In response to our request for our pass, we were informed that there was nothing listed for J.M.J. Center! However, after presenting copies of letters our Cardinal had written in our behalf, we were issued a pass. As we were leaving, we inquired of a Swiss Guard at the desk as to the location assigned us. Looking at our pass, he said we would be seated during the audience and showed us the exact location. Seated! How happy this made us! We would not have to stand as in the past! We were thankful to the Madonna, for had our pass been issued and on file we would perhaps never have had these seats. Truly, the Madonna takes care of everything!

Our pilgrimage group was informed that we would depart the Hotel at 2:15 P.M. even though the audience would not begin until 5:00 P.M. Our hotel was only a few minutes walk from Saint Peter's Square, but we chose to take our bus as we wanted to be the first ones at the gate of entry. The group was instructed to stay very close together and not let anyone come between us so as not to become separated. The Angels certainly were with us for when we arrived at our point of entry, not another soul was to be seen! Quickly we hurried to the gate and there we remained until it opened.

As the hour approached for the Holy Father's audience, some of our pilgrims noticed a young man attempting to get in the front line with our group. Recalling the instructions to remain close together and not become separated, they alerted the assistant group leader. As he approached her, she told him he could not remain with our American group. He left our area quietly but did not leave this particular entry gate.

Soon, the long awaited moment came, the entrance gate was opened and we flew to our seats in the very front row as had been indicated to us by the Swiss Guard. Relief and joy took possession of our tired bodies for we had been standing a few hours. Seated in the front row, we had the ideal place to drape our San Damiano banner.

And then, the long awaited moment was finally upon us! The Holy Father was before us, standing upright in the jeep! He exchanged handshakes and gave his blessing to us and to San Damiano. Our joy was complete for we had had these precious moments with the 'Vicar of Christ!' The jeep proceeded slowly, the Holy Father continuing to greet other pilgrims.

A sudden noise, like that of a gunshot resounded. A group of nuns diagonally across from us and who had a clearer view of the Pope, cried out, "The Holy Father has been shot!" No, it could not be! Yet, incredible as it seemed, our Holy Father had been shot! No, the Madonna would not let him die, she would protect him! Shocked and horrified, such thoughts as these raced through our minds but we believed with deep faith that Heaven would not let him die.

Heading quickly for the nearest exit, the jeep passed by us and in it we saw the slumped bloodstained figure of John Paul II in the arms of those who had been escorting him; his previously joyous countenance was now twisted in pain and assuming a grayish pallor.

Immediately a trembling voice began to recite the Rosary over the loudspeakers and a hushed, shocked crowd responded. - Police, sirens, armed plainclothesmen, helicopters whirring overhead. The assassin was located, encircled by police and captured. - Gradually the crowd dispersed, tears flowing, voices mixed with sadness and anger that such an attempt should be made on the life of the Holy Father.

Returning to our hotel, we listened to our radios for further reports on the Holy Father's condition. At last, an announcement was made: The Holy Father was very seriously injured but he was going to live! Thank you, thank you, Madonna! It all seemed so unreal as we sat listening to

The Holy Father was elected Pope on October 16th, the anniversary date of San Damiano.

Taken by Vatican Photographer on the day of the attempted assassination.

news reports which were interspersed with the hymn 'Christus vincit, Christus regnat, Christus imperat!' - 'Christ comes, Christ rules, Christ conquers!' How many times we had sung this hymn at San Damiano during the preceding weeks!

The following morning, newspaper photos gave us another shock: **The pictured assassin was the very same young man who had tried to attach himself to our group at the entry gate! Had he not been rebuffed by us, he would have been seated with us in the very front row! With such proximity to the Holy Father, what would have been the outcome?**

**Indeed, Christ comes, Christ rules, Christ conquers!**

# Progress at San Damiano

Bishop Antonio Mazza, the present Bishop of the diocese in which San Damiano is located, has made great progress for the Madonna:

✠ He lifted the restriction from Father Pellacani and allowed him to once again offer Mass in public.

✠ Fr. DiCrema has been appointed permanent Pastor at the church of San Damiano. Everyone, including consecrated and religious, can now receive the Holy Eucharist. There is daily Mass with Confessions being heard in Italian or French, the languages spoken by Fr. DiCrema.

✠ An International Youth Pilgrimage Mass is held annually on Church grounds with many priests concelebrating and many thousands of young people in attendance.

✠ Conferences of the Association of the Madonna della Rose have been held in the church hall with Fr. DiCrema opening the Conference.

✠ There is now a medical clinic.

✠ A House for the elderly has been opened. The nurse stationed at the medical clinic visits daily.

✠ Civil authorities have installed a large sign indicating the location of the Shrine of the Madonna delle Rose.

✠ Public sanitary facilities for pilgrims have been completed.

✠ Adult classes are held at the church of San Damiano.

✠ There are Holy Hours for the young people.

✠ Retreats conducted by a Capuchin priest, Fr. Francesco, are held for young people at the site of the future City of Roses.

✠ The Association of the Madonna has donated a new Lector Stand and Baptismal Font to the church and the church interior has been newly painted; old paintings have been restored to their original beauty.

✠ For Fr. Pellacani's Funeral Mass in August of 1989, Bishop Mazza requested all priests present at San Damiano to present themselves at the church in order to concelebrate with him. Cardinal Oddi, the former Apostolic Nunzio of the Vatican, was present at the Mass.

139

**Prayer to the Miraculous Madonna of the Roses**

**O Heavenly Mother, Queen of the Heavens,** Sovereign Lady of men, who has received from God the power and the mission to crush the head of Satan, docile to the invitation of your maternal voice, we hasten to you that you may point out the road of prayer and penance to those who have been led astray and do dispense to the languishing, the graces and prodigies of your sovereign goodness.

**O Merciful Mother,** receive the praises and prayers that your pilgrim children of all the world, oppressed by bitter trials, confidently offer to you.

**O Pure Vision of Paradise,** chase from our minds the darkness of error by the light of **Faith.**

**O Mystical Rose,** revive our tired souls with the heavenly perfume of **Hope.**

**O Inexhaustible Fountain of Salutary Waters,** restore our arid hearts with the divine wave of **Charity.**

We are your children; you comfort us in danger, you sustain us during the struggle. Help us to love and serve Jesus, your Son. Give us an ardent love for your Rosary. Help us to spread devotion to you everywhere; strengthen us so we can live in the state of grace and thus merit eternal joy close to your throne in Heaven ! Amen.

(We approve this prayer and grant a Partial Indulgence to those reciting it.)

Assisi - Italy            **+ Giuseppe Placido Nicolini O.S.B.**
November 8, 1969           **Bishop of Assisi**

The house where Mamma Rosa lived when Our Lady cured her. Photo of Joseph Quattrini, her husband and Aunt Adele.

## Don EDGARDO PELLACANI
N. 1 giugno 1911
M. 2 agosto 1989

*Mamma Rosa's Pastor at the beginning of the apparitions.*

BISHOP ANTONIO MAZZA

The Church of San Damiano

Left: Rosa's mother in the foreground,
her sister, Sister (nun now deceased)
and Rosa to the right of Sister.

Right: Rosa with her family, holding her
youngest son, Pier-Giorgio- her
daughter, Giacomina and her son
Paulo.

Top Photo: Rosa (Center) at 15 yrs. of age.

Bottom Photo: Rosa with her two sisters -
Sister Anna (left) & Sister Pierine

Mamma Rosa's Funeral – September 8th, 1981
Pilgrims came from five continents –
Ten thousand came to pay their respects.

# SAN DAMIANO

## SAINT JOSEPH
## HEAD OF CHRISTIAN FAMILIES

The statue of St. Joseph in the small oratory of St. Joseph, situated in the old Pensione of St. Joseph.

On October 16, 1967, Mamma Rosa said, "Photograph.
"The Madonna has promised a sign." The result was
the above photo.

Statue of Padre Pio adjacent to the Blessed
Garden of the Madonna.
Padre Pio confirmed the authenticity of the
Apparitions of the Madonna to Fr. Pellacani,
Mamma Rosa's Pastor at the beginning of the
Apparitions.

Mamma Rosa's mother and her two sisters, now deceased - Sr. Anna and Sister Pierina

Mamma Rosa with J.M.J. Pilgrimage Chaplains.

Conference room within this building at the 'City of Roses' - there are also apartments for staff of the Association.

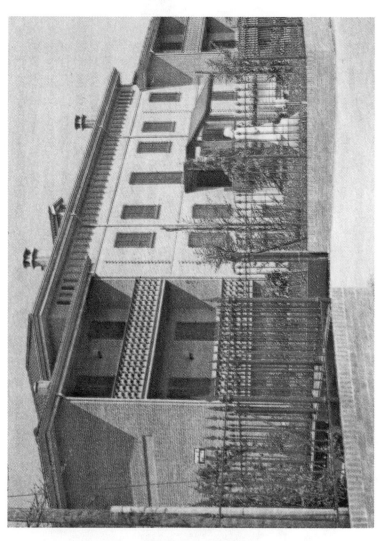

PILGRIM HOUSE
The New House of Saint Joseph

COMMUNITY RESIDENCE

Pensione 'Maria Rosa' owned and operated
by Mr. &Mrs. Mario Basso for pilgrims.

Enclosure of the Blessed Garden
of San Damiano.
Well of the Miraculous Water is
in background.

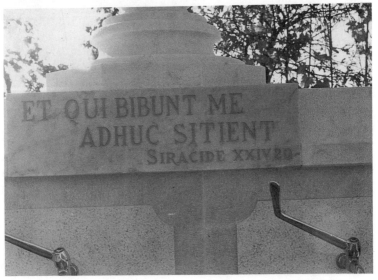

Top Photo:  Marble Fountain from which the
            Miraculous Water is drawn.

Bottom Photo: He who drinks of Me will never
              THIRST.

Canopies for protection from both the hot sun and inclement weather have been erected at the Shrine and at the City of Roses.

Building for use of Youth Pilgrimages at City of Roses provides sanitary facilities and well-equiped kitchen for preparation of meals; power is supplied by solar energy.

Artificial lake in the center of which is a reproduction of the Pieta. Constructed per Rosa's instructions, its environs are the site for a Rosary walk.

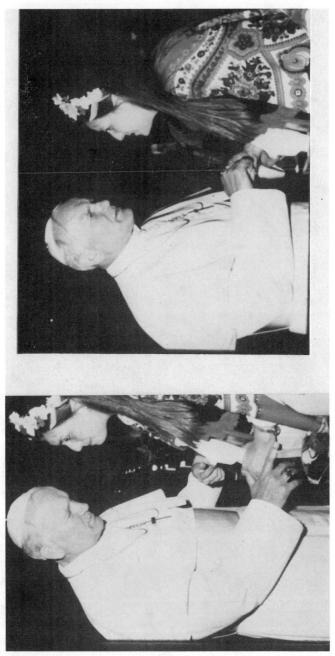

Marie Louise de la Taille of Chile speaks to Our Holy
Father regarding the statement of the then Bishop of
Piacenza. Our Holy Father's response, 'You may go to
San Damiano and tell your priests and Bishops
that they also may go to San Damiano.' She returned
on her next pilgrimage with two Bishops.

J.M.J. Pilgrimage Group at the
New House of St. Joseph at San Damiano.
First Pilgrimage to San Damiano was
in 1971.

Top Photo: Japanese Pilgrims
Bottom: Pilgrims from England

Banner of the J.M.J. American Pilgrims.

The wooden statue of the Miraculous Madonna of the Roses in the larger Chapel of Mamma Rosa's home.

Photo of Irish Pilgrims.

Photo of African Pilgrims.

Pilgrimage group with Mamma Rosa--priest is
Father Pereira from India - a faithful devotee.

A small group of German pilgrims to the left
with their priest.

J.M.J. Pilgrimage Group

The two children (standing next to their mother) made
their First Communion at the Holy House of Loreto.
The Little Flower, St. Therese, received Communion at
the Holy House. Mamma Rosa spoke of the Holy House of
Loreto, denoting much love for the Holy House.

ST. MICHAEL, THE ARCHANGEL
WITH YOUR LIGHT, ENLIGHTEN US!
WITH YOUR WINGS, PROTECT US!
WITH YOUR SWORD, DEFEND US!